DATING, SEX & FRIENDSHIP

An Open and Honest Guide
to Healthy Relationships

Joyce Huggett

INTERVARSITY PRESS
DOWNERS GROVE, ILLINOIS 60515

For Kevin and Christina and their generation.

And with thanks to Joan, who typed the manuscript and gives endless encouragement, and to Phil for the drawing on page 66.

Published in England under the title Just Good Friends? © *Joyce Huggett, 1985*

Published in the United States of America by InterVarsity Press, Downers Grove, Illinois, with permission from Universities and Colleges Christian Fellowship, Leicester, England.

InterVarsity Press is the book-publishing division of Inter-Varsity Christian Fellowship, a student movement active on campus at hundreds of universities, colleges and schools of nursing. For information about local and regional activities, write IVCF, 233 Langdon St., Madison, WI 53703.

Distributed in Canada through InterVarsity Press, 860 Denison St., Unit 3, Markham, Ontario L3R 4H1, Canada.

Unless otherwise stated, quotations from the Bible are from the New International Version, © 1973, 1978, International Bible Society. Used by permission of Zondervan Bible Publishers.

The poems on pages 11-12 and 24-25 are taken from Michael Quoist, Prayers of Life. Used by permission of Sheed & Ward, 115 E. Armour Blvd., P.O. Box 281, Kansas City, MO 64141-0281.

The poem on pages 45-46 is taken from Will You Be My Friend? copyright © 1971 by James Kavanaugh. Reprinted by permission of the publisher. E. P. Dutton, a division of New American Library.

Cover photograph: Steady Cash

ISBN 0-87784-406-2

Printed in the United States of America

Library of Congress Cataloguing in Publication Data
Huggett, Joyce, 1937-
  Dating, sex and friendship.

  1. Youth—Religious life. 2. Dating (Social customs)—Religious aspects—Christianity. 3. Sex—Religious aspects—Christianity. I. Title.
BV4531.2.H8   1985   241'.66   85-19734
ISBN 0-87784-406-2 (pbk.)

17	16	15	14	13	12	11	10	9	8
99	98	97	96	95	94	93	92	91	90

Abbreviations

Bible references which are not taken from the New International Version are quoted with the following abbreviations:

GNB   *Good News Bible,* 1976
JB   *Jerusalem Bible,* 1966
JBP   J. B. Phillips, *Letters to Young Churches,* 1947
LB   *Living Bible,* 1974
RSV   *Revised Standard Version,* 1971

Preface

A friend of mine collects oil paintings. His house is full of them. Another friend collects guns. He has an impressive array. Yet another friend collects fossils. He has created his own museum in the garage of his home.

I am a collector too. As I start this new book on relationships, my collection lies on the desk beside me. It consists of an untidy pile of pieces of paper held together by a large, red, plastic, bulldog-type paper clip. Some scraps of paper measure no more than two inches square. Others bear the marks of being torn from someone's spiral-bound notebook. Others have clearly been tugged from a student's file. Before I begin to write this book, I propose to copy out some of the comments scribbled on these odd pieces of paper. They set the tone and pace for the book I am about to write.

You feel it's right to ask her out. You think she feels the same way but you are not sure. How do you make the move? STALEMATE.

Everyone says that sex is great: a gift from God, but where does this leave the young single person?

At what age should one start dating and what should one do on one's first date?

If the Bible tells us to love everyone and to share our faith with everyone, why do people say that to go out with non-Christians is wrong?

Why is it wrong to have sex before marriage?

How far should Christians go if they don't agree with sex before marriage?

The peer-group pressure to go out with someone is very great. How should a Christian cope with this?

How do I/we keep God at the centre of our relationship when Eros seems so much stronger, more imminent (and infinitely less demanding) than God and is always imperceptibly edging him out?

How much should we pray and do Bible studies together?

How should we relate to others in the fellowship?

You may have guessed by now that my unique collector's item just 'happened'. Whenever David, my husband, and I speak at youth groups or Christian Unions on the subject of boy/girl relationships, we try to leave time for questions, and usually suggest that these questions are submitted in writing to save the questioner embarrassment. Over the years the pile of anonymous questions has snowballed. I tried to respond to some of them in my book *Growing into Love*, but inevitably, since the subject is so vast, many burning issues remained untouched.

This book is a further attempt to respond to questions like the ones I have quoted; questions which continue to perplex young Christians today. I write as a committed Christian who sets out to reflect the Bible's teaching on this complex subject. I also write as one of the many who feel burdened for the marriage relationship in the West and in the East; a relationship which, even among Christians, lies in a sorry state of disrepair.

It is my conclusion that good marriages start in the home when a child observes and enjoys his or her parents' love for one another. It is my conviction, also, that adolescence is the apprenticeship of marriage: as teenagers and young adults learn the difficult art of making in-depth relationships with people of the same sex and people of the opposite sex. And, of course, a further training period comes with courtship, when a young adult experiments with the art form of committed love before and during engagement.

I have already written about Christian marriage in my book *Two into One*. And I have written about the apprenticeship of engagement in *Growing into Love*. This book is not for the married or the engaged. It is for those who ask, like the nurse who wept in my study on one occasion: 'What's wrong with me? I feel so lonely. I really want a boyfriend but I've never had one.' It is for those puzzled by the kind of questions held together by my monster paper clip. It is for those who want to think through the challenge and complexities of sexuality and friendship from a biblical point of view. Whether you are fourteen or eighteen, twenty or twenty-six, and whether you are interested in marriage or equally interested in the art of creative singleness, if the subject of attachments intrigues or bothers you, this book is for you.

One of the problems for the Christian young person living in the West today is that the Bible did not set out to answer the twentieth-century Western questions which cause us so much concern. One of the reasons for this is that the Bible sets out to be neither a sex manual nor a guide to specific relationships; another is, as we shall note later, that in the East when the Bible was written there existed no equivalent to our 'going out' phase in relationships. Girls were often betrothed in infancy and married before their teens. The problems which plague us in the West, and which are beginning to puzzle Christians in the East also, simply did not arise. For this reason, it is not always possible to qualify one's teaching by quoting a specific Bible chapter and verse. What it is possible to do, and what I have tried to do, is to draw on biblical principles and to build on these foundations.

To make good, deep, lasting, worthwhile friendships is rather like rock climbing. It is tough going at times. It is a challenge. It cannot happen without a quota of knocks and bruises. Yet it is fulfilling and rewarding. This book is another attempt to help young Christians negotiate the route marked 'relationships'. It comes with my concern that readers should discover for themselves the truth of that Snoopy poster: 'Thank goodness for people'. It also comes with my prayer that readers should take the necessary risks and embark on the adventure of friendship.

JOYCE HUGGETT

1
Made for Love

'Why doesn't God *do* something? I've told him how desperate I feel, but he just sits there and doesn't do a thing.'

The person who made that complaint to me was not just desperate for love but desperate for a love-partner; someone of the opposite sex to whom he could belong, to whom he could be special, with whom he could create a deep relationship.

Most people experience these longings. From the age of thirteen, or even earlier, they sweep over us from time to time, sometimes overwhelming us and sometimes hurting us with an ache which is so deep and real that it feels like a physical pain. A friend of mine expressed such inner longings in a letter to me once:

'Sometimes, (tonight!), I almost crave for someone who loves me in all ways; mind, body and spirit. I feel I've got so much to give someone, and am so longing to be given to – to have my head cradled and stroked, someone reaching out to *me*, someone telling me they love me. I long for fulfilment sexually – in all aspects, not just physically – though that is a major part – and to be someone else's fulfilment in return. I'm fed up with being single. When I finish writing to you I want to be able to snuggle up with someone more responsive than my hot water bottle.'

Michel Quoist writes similarly, in prayer form: a poignant poem which must have found an echo in many a heart:

> I want to love, Lord,
> I need to love:

All my being is desire;
My heart,
My body,
    yearn in the night towards an unknown one to
    love.
My arms thrash about and I can seize on no object
    for my love.
I am alone and want to be two.
I speak, and no one is there to listen.
I live, and no one is there to share my life.
Why be so rich and have no one to enrich?
Where does this love come from?
Where is it going?
I want to love, Lord,
I need to love.
Here this evening Lord, is all my love unused.[1]

It so happens that the longings so far expressed have all been penned by men. Needless to say, women are not exempt from such yearnings. I think of the attractive girl who admitted her innermost fears to me the other day: 'What's wrong with me? I'm twenty-four and have never had a boyfriend. Why do I feel so lonely?' Or I think of Rachel, the beautiful young girl who confided in me recently: 'I don't seem to be able to make close friendships with anyone – blokes or girls. Other people can do it. Why can't I? I feel so stupid. And what if it goes on like this? As far as I can see, life isn't worth living without warm relationships.'

Rachel was right. Life without warm relationships is drab, empty, painful. We were born for love; made to relate.

The people I have just introduced have voiced some questions which vex many people who hunger after love. In this chapter, we apply ourselves to a few of them. Where does this need for love come from? Why is the accompanying all-consuming desire so hard to handle? Why are we often deprived of the love we feel we need? Did Jesus experience similar longings? If so, how did he deal with them? How can we pattern ourselves on him?

Where does this need for love come from?

I sometimes find myself hurting inside when people share the kind of turmoil contained in the letter I have quoted. It is not unlike the pain and protest I felt when I was out shopping on one occasion. On the pavement in front of me was a mother and her small child. The child was screaming. Instead of consoling her distressed son, the mother lashed out at him, thrashing him not once, but again and again and again until the toddler eventually fell face downwards sobbing, beside himself with shock, fear and, I imagined, very real pain.

We must beware of hitting out at our inner selves like that. It is so easy to do; almost natural. But it is counter-productive. We do it, often, because in the absence in our lives of nurturing relationships, we feel guilty and insecure. We resort to self-blame: 'I shouldn't feel like this'; 'If I was more Christlike I wouldn't need others like this'; 'If I was more mature as a Christian, more spiritual, I should be able to cope without the need for *an* other, someone who is special to me; to whom I am special'. It is when young people make these self-condemning comments to me that I find myself weeping inside. Their presuppositions are completely unbiblical and consequently distinctly harmful. It is hard enough to feel all alone, incapable of making relationships, unlovable. If, on top of that, you blast yourself with self-criticism you are doing as much good (or as much harm) as that mother who deliberately inflicted wounds on her weeping child.

No. Guilt, blaming, self-despising, solve nothing. We must learn to understand where this need for love comes from, and what to do with it.

The Bible unveils the source of need-love in a neat phrase: 'Love comes from God' (1 John 4:7 GNB). The yearning, the deep-felt call of body, heart and mind for the body, heart and mind of another originated in God also. The need for love is not only normal: it is God-implanted, human and spiritual.

The nature of the need
Genesis 2 underlines this fact. Here we catch a glimpse of the Creator surveying and smiling upon his handiwork, the newly--formed universe which exploded into being from his hands.

God approves. The sentence, 'God saw that it was good', occurs like a refrain punctuating the drama of creation. But when God observes the one solitary human being in Paradise, Adam, God concludes, 'It is *not* good for the man to be alone. I will make a helper suitable for him' (Genesis 2:18, italics mine).

'It is not good for the man to be alone.' This profound statement is vital to our understanding of ourselves and human nature in general. God did not intend us to 'go it alone'. God did not even create us equipped to operate solo, to live life in splendid isolation. In fact, even in the perfection of Paradise, man could not cope with his existential loneliness. God created us with an ingrained need for others; for one other, for *an* other.

This observation by the Creator is mind-boggling if you consider the context in which God made it. The disobedience problem had not yet polluted Paradise. God and Adam were still living in uninterrupted harmony. The fall had not yet fouled their fellowship. Even so, without human friendship, Adam suffered an intolerable loneliness.

It would appear, then, that God not only created mankind with a need to relate to others; he also created us with love-needs which he himself chose to meet not with his own presence and comfort, but through people; through a person. What Paul Simon describes in his pain-filled song *I am a Rock* is the antithesis of God's plan. 'I have no need of friendship, Friendship causes pain; Its laughter and its loving I disdain. . .'. John Donne's familiar 'No man is an island' is far more accurate. The truth is that friendship is one of the most precious gifts God entrusts to us. As Margaret Evening observes, 'Life without friendship is hardly life at all.'[2] Or as the writer of Ecclesiastes puts it, 'Two are better than one' (Ecclesiastes 4:9).

The image of God

Why are we so ill-equipped to walk alone? Why does God seemingly stand back and refrain from meeting some of our basic needs for love with his own felt presence? The answer to these questions also lies in Genesis, in a pronouncement made by God in Genesis 1: 'Let us make man in our own image, in the likeness of ourselves. . .' (verse 26 JB).

The Bible gives occasional and fascinating glimpses of life

before 'in the beginning'. John 17:5, for example, refers to the relationship which existed between the Father, the Son and the Holy Spirit before the cosmos was created. John 1:3–4 and Proverbs 8:22 also help us to understand that 'in the beginning' a relationship existed between three co-equal Persons which was characterized by co-operation, communication, commitment and two-directional love : giving love and reciprocal love.

Since man was born reflecting God's nature, it follows that he came complete with the ability to relate to others, co-operate with others, enjoy others, give love to others, and receive love from them. One of man's basic and fundamental needs is the opportunity to give love and receive it. Since man's nature is a miniaturized version of God's, man is lost when he is denied access to a human being with whom he can relate in this way. We each need a soul-friend.

This is why we should never feel guilty when we pine for intimacy. This is why we should never condemn ourselves for craving for closeness. This is why we should not reject ourselves for yearning for relationships. God created us with these desires. As John Powell puts it:

All psychological research has established this fact beyond a doubt. More important than any psychological theory, teaching, or therapeutic technique, that which heals and promotes human change and growth is a one-to-one relationship of love.'[3]

Contrary to the traditional English 'stiff upper lip' mentality and the current American obsession with the Clint Eastwood syndrome, independence is neither biblical nor healing. What we need is *inter*dependence – relationship.

Coping with the pain of waiting
But what if there is an absence of close relationships in your life? What do you do with the deep-seated desire; the pining, the wanting, the waiting a friend once described to me in a letter. 'The ache is deep – and so very real. I know one shouldn't idealize or fantasize and live for an unspecified date in the future when everything *will* be alright. I'm trying not to repress these

feelings, but to hand them to the Lord whilst they're real and present. I know in my heart of hearts that he's in control, his timing is perfect. It's just so hard. And maybe I'm nowhere near ready for marriage or to be trusted with a "lover"?'

It's hard. Very hard. Why is the waiting so hard? Is it because of our natural impatience; our obsession with instant answers; the absence of a plastic card which takes the waiting out of wanting in this area of our life? Is it because of the force of sexual attraction and sexual desire, which we shall look at in detail in the next chapter? Is it because of peer-group pressure or the subtle insistence of the media that to be really happy you must be part of a romantic partnership? Is it the power of unlocked jealousy? 'Everyone I seem to meet is either married or head-over-heels for someone.'

All of these are contributing factors, but if we are to understand ourselves and be patient with ourselves when the desire for a partner nags with the persistent, dull pain of toothache, we need to focus on the major contributing factor: the intimacy crisis. An intimacy crisis can occur at any stage in the life of an adolescent or adult. It arises when there is a scarcity of in-depth relationships in our lives; when the need for closeness feels urgent, or when the apprenticeship of intimacy seems interminably long.

The intimacy crisis

Human beings must have intimacy. Whether we recognize it or not, within each of us there is a powerful longing to create a really deep relationship with at least one other person. For some of us, this yearning is a conscious awareness. For others, the desire is deeply buried in the subconscious and is experienced as a lack in life, an inner emptiness, an absence of meaning and purpose. But this inescapable need for relatedness sets up a striving, an insatiable restlessness. This is particularly prominent in the life of the adolescent and the young adult whose main quest in life, alongside the search for a purpose for living, is this search for greater and greater intimacy in the friendships they forge.

The dictionary defines 'intimacy' in this way: 'close familiarity, a very close friend, euphemism for illicit sexual intercourse'. The thesaurus offers a freight of rich alternatives: 'closeness, trusted, special, devoted, fond, companion, a person with whom one has a mutual attachment, confidante, comrade, fast friend, bosom friend, boon companion, birds of a feather, zealous attachment, concern', to select a few. Eliminate the odd-man-out from the above, 'illicit sexual intercourse' – indeed, eliminate sexual intimacy altogether since we shall be concentrating on that exclusively in the next chapter – and here you have a rag-bag definition of this often misunderstood word, 'intimacy'.

Affection, warmth, touch

Intimacy, like Liquorice Allsorts or Thornton's chocolates, comes in a variety of shapes, textures, colours and tastes; all good, all mouth-watering. It includes the need for touch, warmth, affection, 'we-ness'. This need was highlighted during the war years by some nurses who were working in an emergency hospital ward. To this ward were admitted the babies whose parents had been prematurely and tragically killed. The babies were given adequate and appropriate food, clothes, warmth and shelter. Even so, the mortality rate was alarmingly high. This trend continued until some of the nurses started to cuddle the babies. Every day they would hold them, coo over them, look down on them lovingly, just as their mothers might have done if they had lived. The infants, starved of love and hungry for touch, responded. They thrived. And the nursing profession learned a vital lesson, that food and clothing are not sufficient to meet man's inner needs. Even babies need to *feel* the warmth of a loving human being if they are to survive. What is true of babies is also true of adolescents and adults. We need to feel the warmth of another's care and concern and tenderness. Where such intimacy is not communicated, a vital part of us disintegrates. That is why we strive to build bridges which span the gulf between the island of our existence and the islands of the lives of others. That is why those who fail in this attempt at bridge-building become withdrawn, listless and detached from other people and the world of creativity.

Emotional, intellectual and creative intimacy

But intimacy, as we have seen, is complex. Howard and Charlotte Clinebell describe it helpfully. They speak of *emotional intimacy*, the delight of being tuned in to another's wavelength; *intellectual intimacy*, the stimulus of discovering an affinity with another in the world of ideas; *aesthetic intimacy*, the joy of sharing an experience of beauty with another; *creative intimacy*, the fun and relaxation of relating in experiences of play; *work intimacy*, the togetherness engendered by sharing common tasks; *crisis intimacy*, the bonding which happens when two people tackle problems or handle pain together; *spiritual intimacy*, the wonder and oneness two people experience when they come to the foot of the cross together; *communication intimacy*, the source of all types of intimacy.[4]

During our childhood most of us, if we were fortunate, enjoyed an appreciable degree of such intimacy from our parents or surrogate parents. They cuddled us, read to us, sang to us, explored with us, introduced us to the world of ideas, of nature and creativity. They allowed us to work alongside them in the kitchen, the garden, the workshop. They prayed with us, talked to us and listened to our fears and our tears, our joys and our hopes.

But during pre-adolescence and, in a more marked way, in adolescence, we began to discover the delights of independence; to untie the apron strings which would hold us to our parents inappropriately. We began to reach for intimacy outside of the confines of the immediate family circle.

The problem

The problem is that the quest for extra-familial intimacy and sexual awakening occur simultaneously. Just as we are striving to find a person or persons with whom we can make these new relationships, we are also experiencing new bodily pleasures through our awakened sexual desire, an aspect of growth and maturation which is quite as normal as the persistent and deep-seated desire for closeness. Unfortunately, the media focus attention on the body, on sexual excitation, and this introduces confusion into an already tempestuous situation. Glossy magazines collude with our bodies to persuade us that intimacy is a one-stringed instrument. The subtle implication is that if we indulge in genital sex, sexual intimacy, all the other intimacies will come as part of the package. Through a series of touch-dominated relationships we discover the hollowness of such a belief. In fact, we discover that intimacy is more like a twelve-stringed guitar. It needs each and every string. And each string requires patient and sensitive tuning. We also discover that we are not only hungry for sex but hungry for love; that sex separated from love results not in fulfilment but in disillusionment, even in disgust, self-loathing and scarred memories. We discover that the challenge of the apprenticeship of intimacy, that long, frustrating period from the age of early adolescence right through to the early twenties, is the challenge to integrate developing bodily pleasures and wholesome relationships. And this is no easy task. The apprenticeship is fraught with fear and failure for very many people. And these inner struggles make the waiting period frustrating and hard.

The fear of singleness
One of the fears which adds to the frustration for many young people is the fear of singleness. As one friend of mine put it, 'I'm just not a career girl. I'm the *marrying* kind. If I felt God was asking me to be single for the rest of my life, I'd freak out or something. I just couldn't bear it.'

In today's climate, where there appears to be a worldwide shortage of Christian men, many, many girls harbour such fears and reactions. They gnaw away inside at the same time as they are trying to learn from experience the validity of certain truths : that sexual desire need not control us, it can be transcended, we can control it; that the tenderness and excitement of touch and responsible, truly loving relationships have to be integrated. This fear can still hold us in a vice-like grip at the same time as we are learning, through a variety of maturing friendships, what it means to disclose the hidden self, to give, to be open, to experience ourselves as overflowing, loving people. And, of course, this makes the apprenticeship of intimacy doubly hard.

What makes it even harder is that the craving for intimacy first knocks at the door of our lives at a time of great insecurity and rapid and obvious change: when hormonal changes introduce the onset of menstruation for girls and the unexpected emission of semen in boys; when bodily changes bring about the budding of breasts in girls and the growth of facial hair and the development of the genitals in boys; when emotional changes subject both boys and girls to swing-boat changes of mood, the apparent inability to control these powerful moods, and the phase of the obsessional crush either for a person of the same sex or for a person of the opposite sex.

Why the deprivation?

As though the apprenticeship was not sufficient challenge in itself, like the young man whose complaint introduced this chapter, we often suffer the sorrow of being deprived of love. We must now consider why this is.

Christians, I find, seem to resort to blaming God when there is a deficiency of love in their lives. They shake their fists at God, rail at him, and forget that we are not God's robots, nor are we puppets on God's string whose lives are manipulated by him. God does not pull a string here and a string there to solve our friendship problem. No. He has created us as persons with the freedom of choice: a choice he expects us to exercise in the realm of relationships.

One of the reasons why we suffer from a lack of love is that we pin all our hopes and expectations of intimacy on *one* person. We expect that one person to satisfy all our needs: intellectual, recreational, spiritual, social. And we fail to recognize that this all-sufficient person does not exist. If these innermost needs of ours are to be met, they must be met through several persons. By burdening *one* friend with such high hopes and expectations we are endangering the relationship, probably strangling it.

There is another reason for the lack of love we experience. It is the fear I mentioned earlier. This fear and insecurity clogs up our lives in the same way as dirt clogs the carburettor of a car. Our life refuses to run smoothly. It jerks and jolts through circumstances and has a disconcerting habit of cutting out, emotionally speaking, at embarrassing moments and in irritating ways. And we seek to escape from the closeness we crave rather than take the risk of relating to others.

Did Jesus experience these feelings?

Jesus demonstrated, among other things, certain ways of forging firm friendships. How did he go about it? Did he experience the same feelings as we do?

Jesus was human. Jesus was sexual. Jesus was tempted. The Bible makes this comforting fact crystal clear. 'Our High Priest is not one who cannot feel sympathy for our weaknesses. On the contrary, we have a High Priest who was tempted in every way that we are, but did not sin' (Hebrews 4:15–16 GNB).

Jesus was tempted in *every* way that we are. Try to drink in the relevance of this verse to our present study. Among Jesus' followers were many women, some of them possibly extremely attractive. Isn't it probable that, although Jesus knew that celibacy was the Father's will for him, from time to time feelings of loneliness would sweep over him? The writer to the Hebrews suggests that Jesus identified with our humanity fully. Thanks be to God we do not have to refer to an asexual High Priest but to one who, when he clothed himself with our humanity, became a man also with all the joys and tensions that that involved.

And the mystery of Jesus is that this Man above all men shows us how to achieve true intimacy, how to be fulfilled in our relationships, and how to be fulfilled in our loving even though we may never marry. In Paradise, God alleviated man's aloneness with a woman. In Jesus, God introduces a new model to meet our need for love. The model includes a perfect interweaving of dependence on ourselves, on God and on other people.

Jesus' model of friendship

Although the prototype for human friendship provided for us by Jesus has particular relevance for people who are not married, the qualities of Jesus' style of friendship apply equally, of course, to that unique friendship of marriage: the husband-wife friendship. But in listing some of the ingredients of Jesus' friendship here, I have in mind those readers whose quest for intimacy is pressing, urgent. My advice would be: cut your life to the pattern of Jesus.

We have made frequent mention of the word intimacy already in this chapter. In his farewell conversation with his disciples (John 14–17), Jesus defines intimacy. Intimacy is being inside of your friend, and having him inside of you (John 15:4–5). Jesus is not describing sexual fusion here, the coming together of two bodies. He is describing emotional oneness, the kind of love we first learn at the toddler level when we grow sufficiently certain of mother's love and presence to be separated from her for a period of time, to stay with a baby-minder or to attend playschool.

Intimacy is love trusting

Donald Goergen, in his illuminating study of John 14–17[5], points our attention to other essential ingredients of Jesus' style of friendship.

Friendship for Jesus included complete *openness and self-disclosure*. Indeed, in John 15:15 Jesus provides a definition of friendship. Friendship is making everything known to your friend. It is sharing. It is relating to him everything the Father has revealed to you. Thus the friendship modelled by Jesus is emotional closeness, being in tune with your friend; intellectual closeness, enjoying the world of ideas; and spiritual closeness, delighting in the Father's love.

Friendship for Jesus did not happen willy-nilly, by chance. He chose his friends (John 15:16). This element of controlled choice is an important lesson for us to learn. Jesus did not open himself in the self-revealing way I have described to everyone he happened to meet. Neither did he unveil his innermost secrets to all those who would have befriended him. No. Jesus was careful: selective. Wise. From the multitude, he selected seventy. From the seventy he selected twelve with whom he lived and talked and walked and shared, with whom he enjoyed intimacy. Out of this group of twelve, he made a further selection of three: Peter, James and

John. And from the three emerged one : John, the beloved. If we seek intimacy, we must follow the example of Jesus. Be selective. Let this choosing arise from our prayer. After all, who we are and what we become depends largely on the people who love us and with whom we spend our time.

Self-sacrifice, joy, pain
One of the stunning qualities of real friendship is *self-sacrifice*. In Jesus' terms, complete self-giving is what friendship is. A friend is someone who lays down his life for us, and for whom we lay down our lives. In true friendship there can be no holding back. This is why the element of choice is vital and pressing. We cannot love everyone in this costly way.

Most of us want the riches of friendship without paying the price. Alas! This is not possible. There is a high cost to true loving. But it produces *dividends of joy*. Jesus wanted to make his friends happy (John 15:13). He believed that by sharing his joy with them, his own joy would be rounded off, complete (John 17:13).

He was equally aware of the presence of *pain* in friendship. He warned, for example, that the pain of separation stings (John 16:20).

Compassion, concern, non-possessiveness
Was it the inevitable intertwining of joy and pain in friendship which gave birth to Jesus' *concern* for his friends? We are not told. What we do know is that this concern runs through his friendships like a life-giving vein. He was concerned for their physical well-being, their emotional security and supremely for their spiritual well-being (John 17:11–12). His deepest expressed desire and burden is that his friends should remain true to God their Father. Was this the guiding principle which governed his behaviour, which prompted him to accept full responsibility for those he gathered under his wing? Again, we are not told. But if this aim becomes the gauge of our behaviour, we will not abuse this most precious gift of friendship.

Despite the depth of his concern for his friends, Jesus' friendship was never claustrophobic, exclusive or possessive.

No. It was characterized by an *outward orientation* and a superlative *generosity*. Jesus, far from being jealous if his friends loved one another, actively encouraged them to do so. Indeed, the sign that they were his friends was to be this mutual free-flowing love: 'All men will know that you are my disciples if you love one another' (John 13:34). What is more, Jesus longed that his friends should become fulfilled people by discovering and pursuing their calling (John 15:16). Real friendship is this: not preventing your friend's growth, stifling his God-given ambition, or blocking his path to a fruitful ministry, but standing with him, helping him discover his gifts and his calling and then offering encouragement, prayer and support: 'You can do it.' Such friendship emulates the friendship of Jesus. It is liberating and fulfilling.

Donald Goergen concludes, and I agree, 'There is no greater love than the friendship of which Jesus speaks. The effects of this kind of relationship: the deepest and most intimate union imaginable.'[6] As Jesus himself said, it is analogous to the Father's relationship with the Son (John 15:9).

Our deepest need, mankind's deepest need, is to overcome our separateness, to take risks of friendship so that eventually we enjoy the riches of intimacy. The challenge is to model ourselves on the life of Jesus, to be transformed into his likeness by the Holy Spirit. But it takes time. In our quest for a Christlike balance between self-sufficiency, dependency on God and on others, we shall fall many times. Like Michel Quoist, this failure will cause us to cry out:

> 'I have fallen, Lord,
> Once more.
> I can't go on, I'll never succeed.
> I am ashamed, I don't dare look at you. . .'

And the Lord will answer:

> 'Come, son, look up.
>   Isn't it mainly your vanity that is wounded?
> If you loved me, you would grieve, but you would
>   trust. . .

Ask my pardon
And get up quickly.
You see, it's not falling that is the worst,
But staying on the ground!'[7]

Notes for chapter one

1. Michel Quoist, *Prayers of Life* (Gill & Son, 1963), p.38.
2. Margaret Evening, *Who Walk Alone* (Hodder and Stoughton, 1974), p.38.
3. John Powell, *The Secret of Staying in Love* (Argus, 1974), p.44.
4. Howard J. Clinebell and Charlotte H. Clinebell, *The Intimate Marriage* (Harper and Row, 1970), pp. 37–38.
5. Donald Goergen, *The Sexual Celibate* (Seabury Press, 1974).
6. *The Sexual Celibate*, p.164.
7. Michel Quoist, *Prayers of Life*, pp. 104–106.

2
Be Holy *and* Sexual

A whole cluster of intimacies contribute to worth-while friendships. We examined some at length in chapter one. But we omitted the one which presents most people with most problems: sexual intimacy. The omission was deliberate on my part, not because it is of no importance, but because it is of vital importance. It is so important that in this chapter we shall talk about things sexual to the exclusion of everything else.

Although whole books have now been devoted to the subject of sex, there remains an urgent need to tidy up the existing chaotic aftermath of the sexual revolution of the '60s. Like shopkeepers clearing up the High Street after a week-end of looting, we shall attempt to bring order out of confusion, beauty from what seems like destruction.

In order to effect this sexual clean-up, it is necessary to consider certain questions. The answers affect our attitudes, our behaviour and our emotions. The questions span such broad considerations as: What does popular Christian opinion have to say about sex? What is God's verdict? What are we to understand by this over-used word 'sexuality'? How can we adequately accept and appropriately express our sexuality? What is Jesus' example?

Beliefs about sex
Beliefs about sex lie in the church today like layers of assorted biscuits in a tin. Some Christians still hold an ultra-pessimistic view. For them, sex is still the great unmention-able. Others have shaken off the taboos of the past and

adopted the sex ethic of the permissive society in which we live. Yet others are beginning to give thanks to God for sex, recognizing that it is one of his gifts. But some still practise a kind of dualism. As one young Christian voiced it recently, 'I can see that sex within marriage is desirable, possibly even beautiful. But as a single person, I've always believed I had to be asexual until I'm married.'

To be human is to be sexual. No-one can be sexless. I propose, therefore, to look at some of the more common myths about sex; to highlight them so that we can place them alongside the truths which we find in the Bible.

A blight on human nature
Some Christians believe that the sexual surges which pulsate through our bodies are marks of man's disobedience, man blemished by the fall, the fleshly lusts Peter speaks of in 1 Peter 2:11. Such Christians cannot imagine that Adam and Eve might have enjoyed sex-play in Paradise. They find it difficult to accept that God looked on the naked bodies of the man and woman he had made genitally equipped to enjoy playing with each other, and that he labelled this artistry 'good'. The prevailing mood which surrounds human sexuality for such people is not celebratory, a sign of wholeness or healthy aliveness. No. It is finger-wagging reproachfulness, condemnation; in the eyes of some, even evil.

This negativism which has percolated through the Christian world for centuries fills our minds and affects our attitudes more deeply than we realize. Even though, in our heads, we believe we have smashed the 'sex-is-shameful' belief so that it lies in tiny pieces on the ground, our reactions and attitudes reflect our reluctance to believe that God was the architect of sexual sensations, sexual activity and indeed, the human body with its sexual identity.

God underlined this for me just before I began writing this book. I was in Cyprus, soaking up the sun, praying about this book and writing Scripture Union notes on the subject of the Second Coming of Christ. One evening, while I was in the bath, loud noises startled me. It sounded as though all the residents of the high-rise block of flats where we were staying had congregated in the flat above ours and were hammering on the walls and ceilings of our apartment. When the bath began to move and the walls to tremble, I called out in terror, 'What's happening?' No-one answered, so I leapt out of the bath and ran to the lounge in search of my husband. As I ran my mind flashed to my Scripture Union notes; to my assertion that Jesus had promised to return one day. 'Perhaps he's come?' The initial sense of excitement evaporated as I looked down at my naked body. 'Oh no! He can't choose *this* minute. I'm naked. And I'm still dripping wet.'

Since that evening, our first experience of an earthquake, I've asked myself many times why I was so reluctant to face my Maker in a state of undress. I know in my head that God created my body, that he would not be embarrassed to see me naked. But do I really acknowledge this fact with my emotions? I hate to admit it, but my emotions and my head were out of alignment. Although I had been asking others to accept their bodies and their sexuality as God-given gifts I had not reached that degree of maturity myself. Sex can be embarrassing, a threat, an unbearable tension.

Even in the sex-saturated society in which we live today, for many Christians the very word 'sex' is embarrassing. I think of the young Christian who once came to see me to talk about the sexual struggles which plagued her. In the middle of the conversation, she blurted out, 'This conversation will have to stop. It's making me feel physically sick. It's just not wholesome to talk about sex.' It was not that the conversation was in any sense smutty or distasteful. It was just that she could not hear to think of herself as a sexual human being.

For such Christians, the very presence of powerful chemical reactions surging through their body poses a threat. The spontaneous, tantalizing, uninvited biological urges which clamour for attention in all of us at one time or another, crowd out the presence of Christ and cancel out all attempts to pray and worship. As one student expressed it to me: 'You see an attractive girl in church and you're finished. You look away – at the stained glass windows or the organist or the preacher, but your concentration has gone. There's no way you're going to experience the presence of God. You might just as well go home or go for a walk as try to be part of what's going on round you.'

When biological urges compete so successfully with the spiritual disciplines which feed our soul, it is easy to be beguiled into believing that sex is an all-conquering demon; that when it beckons you have no option but to capitulate to its demands.

Sex gives rise to fear, anxiety, guilt
Sex is not only an embarrassing factor in our personality, a tigress which seems to defy all attempts we make to hold the controls of our behaviour, but, for some, it seems to become an unbearable tension, giving rise to fear, anxiety and guilt. Teenage boys, for example, can become very anxious when 'wet dreams' begin, particularly if no-one has explained to them that this is a normal part of the maturing process. Similarly girls can be full of fear when their periods begin. Some even wonder whether they might be seriously ill, or bleed to death.

Many are plagued with unexpressed guilt about their first physical encounters with the opposite sex:

'I remember my first boyfriend. I was only fourteen. We kissed and fondled each other. I liked it. But I was frightened too. I used to pray every night, "Lord, show me if I'm displeasing you." But there was no-one I could talk to about it so I went on not knowing if I was sinning or not, so always feeling vaguely guilty.'

Sex: a force to be reckoned with, repressed or suppressed
Because sex is such a fearsome animal its influence, in the eyes of some, needs to be suppressed or repressed. 'I don't think it should even be talked about. You just don't know what you'll encounter if you once start talking about these things.' Suppression, consciously forcing sexual awakening into a kind of internal Pandora's box and firmly and stubbornly sitting on the lid, is useless. It is not unlike putting a

bomb in the box and sitting on it. And repression, blocking out your sexual desires so effectively that you pretend to be sexless, is worse. It is ineffective, but also harmful because it's unreal. Sex is so powerful that it will find some way of expressing itself, maybe even through perversion. Sex is an essential part of you, vital to your emotional growth. Cut it off, like amputating a limb, and your maturing never comes to full fruition. Your growth is stunted.

The tragedy is that many Christians deny their sexuality because they misunderstand the value of this part of their personality. They mistake normal, powerful, bodily sensations for lust. As we shall go on to observe later, these strong biological undercurrents *can* sweep us into lustful thought-patterns or behaviour, but of themselves they are not lustful, they are an appetite, like hunger. An appetite, of itself, is not immoral but neutral.

Sex is good, a panacea for all woes
Many Christians today, as I have said, now consider this sexual negativism to be outmoded. They have exchanged these views for more fashionable garments. They rejoice in the bodily pleasures which accompany sexual awakening, but they allow this pleasure to become the guiding principle of their lives. Instead of learning that any emotion can be controlled by the will which co-operates with the Holy Spirit of God, they play into the hands of the goddess of lust and abandon themselves to her. Like many of their non-Christian counterparts, they swallow the twentieth-century lie: that sexual experiences alleviate aloneness, that sex is the panacea for all woes. They look to sexual experience for emotional completion and wonder why a series of sexual encounters leaves them feeling, not complete, but drab, jaded, abandoned, soiled.

What is sexuality?
I have written enough to show that the Christian world is still bemused by this force we call sex. We must now move on to enquire what this word really means.

Perhaps the most satisfactory description of sex is this: sex is a mystery. A mystery is something we are incapable of understanding with our tiny, finite minds. Sex is one of the parts of our being human which we shall never fully fathom. Even so, we need to try to understand it, so we must search for definitions.

Sex, as we have already observed, is a biological awakening; what Lewis Smedes calls 'a glandular urge'.[1] As such it is natural, a part of our make-up, designed by God. The ability to be attracted to the opposite sex was implanted in us by God. At least, that is the way I understand Genesis 2:25. The ability to be fascinated by the curves and personality of the opposite sex was also built in by God way back in Genesis 1:27–28. And the ability to feel drawn to another for sexual contact, in much the same way as iron filings are drawn to a magnet, was dreamed up by God, created by him. Sexual excitation, like the sex drive, was God's idea. Hormones and erections, tender breasts and ejaculations and the stomach somersaulting with desire, were God's brain-children.

Sex is natural, biological. It is also an appetite: a chemical reaction conveying an urgent message, like hunger. This appetite is at its most intense, particularly for boys, between the ages of sixteen and eighteen. Appetites are strange phenomena. They clamour to be satisfied immediately. But if you fast, you soon discover that appetites need not control you. You can control them. When you abstain from food, at first your tummy protests, you feel hungry, even faint. But as the fast continues you feel less hungry, not more. The same is true if you diet sensibly. You find you want less food, not more.

Exactly the same principle applies with sexual fasting. If you give in to sexual demands, your body, like a tyrant, will demand more and more. The desire becomes insatiable. But if you observe a sexual fast or a strict sexual diet, the appetite shrinks to a manageable size. You gain the mastery.

Sex: a reunion, a wholesome, clean drive

The quest for a fuller definition of sex is fascinating. One of the assurances it brings is that sex is neither dirty nor evil. How can it be? As we have already seen and shall go on to emphasize, God created it. And Timothy reminds us that nothing created by God could be unwholesome. 'Everything that God has created is good; nothing is to be rejected, but everything is to be received with a prayer of thanks. . .' (1 Timothy 4:4 GNB). Or as the psalmist expresses it,

> You made all the delicate, inner parts of my body, and knit them together in my mother's womb. Thank you for making me so wonderfully complex! It is amazing to think about. Your workmanship is marvellous. . . .You were there while I was being formed in utter seclusion! (Psalm 139:13–15 LB).

When we begin to realize this, it is as though the veil is lifted from our eyes and we see human sexuality for what it is: a necessity. Without the sex drive, men and women would not be propelled towards one another in that quest for intimacy we examined in the first chapter of this book. The sexual drive is the motor which moves the machine of our life towards this fascinating other person who is equipped, not just to fulfil our genital needs, but to give us love and be loved by us, to give us trust and be trusted by us, to give us a sense of belonging and, in turn, to find their sense of belonging in us: in our bodies and in emotional oneness.

Sex is the means whereby a mysterious fusion can take place. Sex is not so much a union as a *re*union. God took Adam, the one, and made two from the one. But they did not remain separate for long. They came back together again. They were reunited. This reunion at its best spells completeness: physical, emotional and spiritual.

Sex, not just genitality

But sex must never be thought of simply in terms of hormones and orgasms, sex organs and sex urges. Sex encompasses a breadth of meaning which includes this genitality and goes beyond it. We have so far used the term 'sex' to describe sexual intercourse, sexual attraction, genital desire. We must now go on to consider the social dimension of sexuality, the non-genital aspect of sex which lies as much at the core of our personality as this urgent longing for bodily fusion.

Donald Goergen describes non-genital sex in this way:

> The social dimension of our sexuality consists in the tender relationships we experience. It is the affectionate, compassionate, and tender side of sexuality. Affection, compassion, tenderness, warmth are rooted in sexuality and expressive of sexuality, although not specifically genital. . . . Sexuality includes the whole area of our emotional warmth as human beings.[2]

Goergen goes further and concludes:

> The tender and compassionate person is a person who has reached sexual maturity. As long as we do not feel comfortable with our biology and physiology, we are not going to be able to socialize our sexuality. . . . If the genital side of sexuality is repressed it is going to lead to an effectively inhibited person.[3]

In trying to define sexuality, then, if we are to be accurate in our thinking we must hold two concepts in tension: the genital or sensual and the social or affectionate. Whenever we use the overworked word 'sexual' we must learn to distinguish in our minds just what we mean by this term. Often we use the word sexual when we mean genital: sexual intercourse when we mean genital intercourse, sexual intimacy when we mean genital intimacy, sexual desire when we mean the longing for bodily closeness.

God's verdict on sex

With this dual meaning in our minds, we turn to the question of sex from God's perspective. Does God really like sex: the emotional *and* the genital expression of oneness? In answering that question, few of us would query whether God applauds warmth and tenderness, kindness and patience between persons. We know from 1 Corinthians 13 that this is central to true intimacy. But does God really approve of genitality? Did he really intend Adam and Eve to enjoy the bodily pleasures sexual excitation brings? Did he really invent orgasms, the genital pleasure which brings contentment and peace to married partners? Or were these pleasures stumbled on by men and women? Are they, perhaps, unknown to God? For adequate answers to these questions, we must search the Scriptures.

God is pro-sex

The more I delve into the Bible, the more convinced I become that God is pro-sex. If you are looking for anti-sex propaganda you will not find it in the pages of the Bible. A quick survey of key passages from the Old and New Testaments establishes this fact.

As we observed in chapter one, Genesis 2:18–25 is a good place to start. Here God deliberately and intentionally creates for man a companion with a separate sexual identity, which the man finds attractive and magnetic. Different. God creates their differences, not for separateness, but for oneness. God intended that the two should be reunited so that the needs created by their deep loneliness would be met in one another. This fellowship and unity included all the intimacies we observed in chapter one and also extended to the genital. Genesis 2:25 is an appreciation of the human body: 'The man and the woman were both naked, but they were not embarrassed' (GNB). It was not just that embarrassment had not entered Paradise. It was far more positive than that. They celebrated. They delighted in one another, physically and emotionally and in the presence of God. And God saw that it was good.

I make that claim, not because of chapter and verse from Genesis, but because of the Song of Solomon. If ever extravagant language was used to describe sensuous love-play it is used in this book of the Bible. As in Genesis, the language used is celebratory. God does not have a down on sex, he created men and women genitally equipped to lead one another into transports of delight. In the context of committed marital love, this is the pleasure he wants them to give to one another.

The New Testament takes up this joyful theme. When Jesus is asked questions concerning marriage and sex, he reminds his hearers of the basic principles outlined in Genesis: sex and marriage are God's gifts, planted in Paradise. 'Haven't you read the scripture . . . in the beginning the Creator made people male and female? And God said, ". . . the two will become one" ' (Matthew 19:4–6 GNB). In other words, 'Don't you understand that from the beginning God intended that men and women should be attracted to each other; they should satisfy one another?' And Paul, who is often accused of being negative about sex, underlines the God-givenness of marital union. In Ephesians 5 he initiates an amazing analogy. Marital oneness which includes the sexual union is not unlike the relationship which exists between Christ, the bridegroom, and his bride, the church: close, permanent, binding. No-one can find a higher, more wholesome picture of the love of man and woman than that.

It follows, from what we have observed, that God's view of sex is not belittling, degrading or negative, as we shall see again in chapter five. On the contrary, far from seeing sex as a horrid by-product of the fall, the Bible sees it as natural, designed, ordained and blessed by God. These truths explode most of the myths we have pin-pointed already in this chapter. So we must go on to ask why we in the church are still in such a hopeless muddle about sex.

Man's muddle

In an earlier book, *Two into One* (chapter nine), I tried to show how the pessimistic view of sex crept into the church: through the anti-sex stance adopted by the early Fathers. After Ephesians 5 and the superlative image of genital intercourse Paul used, the pendulum swung from positive to negative. By the fourth century the view that genital intercourse is synonymous with original sin was firmly established. Even though this so-called Christian teaching about sex was unbiblical, it formed the basis of the church's propaganda for centuries.

The 'sex is filthy' myth put down long and sturdy roots and pushed up prolific and growing shoots, and although various attempts were made to axe the tree, they made as much or as little impression as assaulting a giant oak with a rubber axe. Then came the sexual revolution of the 1960s. This exposed the tree for what it was: a sham, a tree sporting the semblance of life and one which was rotten at the core.

Unfortunately, the sexual revolution was no more biblical than the teaching it was trying to undermine. It replaced negativity towards sex with idolization and prohibition with permissiveness and glamourization. It forgot or ignored the fact that, although sex is natural, like every other part of our personality it is also shot through with sin. This huge swing of the pendulum, with its invitation, indeed emphasis, on sexual licence or so-called freedom, resulted in untold harm. It is only now, twenty years later, that journalists are recording the degree of the damage. To quote just one:

> The letting down of barriers in the 1960s seemed to some of us a glorious revolution. Now, as we see the carnage that has been wrought in the lives of so many adolescent girls, those of us who hailed the loosening up of the sexual rules as a triumph against hypocrisy, have sadly begun to think again.[4]

Whenever the pendulum of popular opinion swings from left to right and back again, people are inevitably caught in the middle, still working out their own viewpoint. This is the situation which faces us today. And whatever the Bible may say about the context of the full genital expression of sex being marriage, and however persuasive people's warnings about promiscuity and genital licence are, the door has been swung open and the wild horse has bolted. As we have seen, sex is not just about attitudes and emotions. Sex is energy. Sex can be an obsession. Sex can be compulsive. To add to the problem, man has an urgent need to comform, a fear of being the odd-man-out.

The need to conform
Conformity is the need to be like everyone else, to behave as they behave, to think as they think, to dress as they dress.

Conformity is the fear of being different from the group, the fear that if you reject commonly-held ideas you yourself will be rejected, and the fear of being laughed at. In the West today, particularly among adolescents and young adults, the pressure to conform is enormous. A girl who once confessed her sexual sin to me put the situation succinctly. 'Oh yes! I know what the Bible says about sleeping around, but I just dismissed that as old-fashioned. After all, everybody's doing it. Why should I be different? My friends just wouldn't understand. They'd mock.'

It is this pressure, coupled with the overwhelming power-fulness of the sexual drive, which sometimes pushes Christians into behaving promiscuously and unbiblically. Christians, like others influenced by the media, friends and society, become sexually active, not necessarily because they want genital kicks, but because they do not know how to abstain. This same pressure paralyses others, like the person I've already mentioned who concluded: in the face of all these pressures, there's only one solution, not to conform but to pretend: to become sexless.

For the committed Christian, neither of these options is ideal or biblical. Instead, we must learn both to accept our sexuality as God-given and to express it appropriately. We shall look at the nuts and bolts of the outworking of this ethic in more detail in chapters five and six. Here, we content ourselves with the example Jesus set before us and aim to pattern our lives on his example and teaching.

Jesus' pattern

We have seen that the sex drive is as bewildering and exciting as driving a Mercedes on the motorway when you are used to driving a Renault 4. It wants to go places fast, and you want to be taken with it. We have to come to terms with the fact that these desires of themselves are not sinful. But those of us who are honest know how very easily they catapult us into sinful fantasies, sexploitation and downright, common lust. Sex may not be sinful of itself but we know that more than any other human appetite it incites us to sin. So what did Jesus do about his sexuality?

Jesus? Sexual? Yes. As we saw in chapter one, Jesus
identified fully with our humanity. He is not the asexual
person some people seem to believe him to be. John spells
out this fact in the first chapter of his Gospel. 'The Word
(Jesus) became flesh.' Flesh! Jesus was not just skin and
bones. Surely, if this word 'flesh' means anything it means
that Jesus became sexually aware like any other teenage boy;
that he knows how it feels to experience the bodily changes of
adolescence and almost certainly experienced the emotions
felt by every normal man.

If this is so, what can we learn from him?

Of one thing we can be certain: Jesus did not conform to
the cultural norm. He was unafraid to swim against the tide.
I say this for two reasons. One, because the cultural norm
was for men to marry and Jesus remained single. Two,
because the cultural norm was for married men to have
children by their wives and genital pleasure with a mistress,
but Jesus modelled sexual celibacy. Just as Jesus refused to
bend under the pressure of the cultural norm, so must we. As
Paul puts it, we must not let the world around us squeeze us
into its own mould (Romans 12:1 JBP). Rather, we must
allow God to re-mould our minds.

Jesus was not a conformist, but neither did he repress or
suppress his sexuality. No. He allowed the social side of his
sexuality full and free expression. Thus he developed warm
and tender relationships with men and women alike. The
Gospels lead us to believe that John and Peter, Lazarus,
Martha, Mary and others of his friends were really important to him. We know that Jesus expressed his affection
through touch and allowed others to touch him. This does
not mean that he behaved promiscuously. On the contrary,
Jesus was so much master of himself that he could re-channel
his emotional drives into the ability to make lasting friendships. In Jesus, we watch an amazing miracle unfold before
our eyes. In Genesis, God proclaimed that it is not good for
man to be alone. God provides man with a source of sexual
intimacy in the fullest sense of that word: woman. But Jesus
shows that a man can be alone, genitally deprived, yet
emotionally fulfilled; that in his state of singleness he can

enjoy maturity and wholeness. In this, as so often, Jesus turns our expectations on their heads. In short, the man Jesus shows us how to be thoroughly holy and thoroughly sexually aware.

What this surely means, then, is that even though we are absorbingly sexual people – sexual through and through like Jesus – we must learn to feel at home with our bodies, our erotic desires, our pounding hearts. These biological urges can become the spring-board for outgoing, affectionate friendships which do not stoop to treating the bodies of others as toys. We need to achieve a self-awareness, even a body-awareness, which recognizes the changes that are happening inside us, at adolescence and every time we love someone deeply, which refuses to despise these reactions or think of them as enemies, but rather views them as part of God's amazingly fertile creativity. The result is a miraculous unfolding of that mysterious thing we call personhood. In other words, like Jesus, we must learn to integrate the two halves of sexuality, the social and the genital, and flatly refuse the genital permission to rule the roost.

It would be easy to dismiss all this with a shrug of the shoulders and the bleat, 'Well! It's all right for Jesus. He was perfect.' Yes. He was. But he learned the obedience of perfection through the things which he suffered (Hebrews 5:8). Did this suffering include the mental torment of knowing that some women were drawn to him by the magnetism of erotic love? Does it mean that he suffered the anguish of finding some women attractive, while being denied the opportunity to express these strong feelings? The Gospels do not tell us. I personally believe that Jesus' life, sexually speaking, was as much a potential collision course as our own, that he confronted such temptations head-on. But he never sinned. That is amazing.

And yet. On the first Good Friday, soldiers led him to the cross. There, under the blazing heat of the relentless sun, he died a cruel death. Crucifixion. Jesus hung on that cross because you have sinned: because I have sinned. We have failed in many ways. We have failed sexually in thought, word and deed. When Jesus hung there, our sins were transferred to him. Because he suffered to the bitter end, he dealt the final death-blow to sin's power. However powerful the sex drive within us is, we no longer have to capitulate. Because Jesus died, because Jesus rose again, we do not have to suffer the indignity of a sexuality which is stained. If we are in Christ we have within us another more powerful dynamic: the power which raised Jesus from the dead. If we draw on this power, we can experience the richness of the kind of non-genital relationship we witness at the Garden tomb on Resurrection Day. Mary, sick with grief and sick with love, weeps at the graveside of the One she loves. He comes to her. In one warm, tender, emotionally-charged word, he greets her: 'Mary!' Do they embrace? No. Gently and kindly he refuses her permission to depend on touch. Instead, they enjoy the oneness of an indestructible friendship.

C.S. Lewis captures the nuances and frolic so well:

'Oh, Aslan!' cried both children, staring up at him. . . .
'Aren't you dead then, dear Aslan?' said Lucy.
'Not now,' said Aslan. . . .
'Oh, you're real, you're real! Oh, Aslan!' cried Lucy and both girls flung themselves upon him and covered him with kisses. . . .
'Oh, children,' said the Lion, 'I feel my strength coming back to me. Oh, children, catch me if you can!' He stood for a second, his eyes very bright, his limbs quivering, lashing himself with his tail. Then he made a leap high over their heads and landed on the other side of the Table. Laughing, though she didn't know why, Lucy scrambled over to reach him. Aslan leaped again. A mad chase began. Round and round the hill-top he led them, now hopelessly out of their reach, now letting them almost catch his tail, now diving between them, now tossing them in the air with his huge and beautifully velveted paws, and catching them again, and now stopping unexpectedly so that all three of them rolled over together in a happy laughing heap of fun and arms and legs. It was such a romp as no one ever had except in Narnia; and whether it

was more like playing with a thunderstorm or playing with a kitten Lucy could never make up her mind.[5]

This refreshingly different description of the kind of relationships Jesus enjoyed (for in Narnia, Aslan the lion represents the Messiah) sums up much of what we have been saying in the last two chapters. Jesus was so wholly human, so comfortably masculine, that relationships with him could be warm and tender, affectionate and fun, serious and relaxing. Real. With Jesus as your friend you felt you mattered. With Jesus as your friend you had someone who understood you. With Jesus as your friend you never knew what would happen next, but you did know that whatever it was it would be good.

This is sexuality at its richest, at its most profound. It leaves me panting for breath, asking the question, 'How can *we* make relationships like that?' That is the subject of the next chapter. For a closer study of the vexed question: 'Are we allowed *any* form of genital expression of love before we're married?' we must wait until chapters five and six.

Notes for chapter two

1. Lewis Smedes, *Sex in the Real World* (Lion, 1976).
2. Donald Goergen, *The Sexual Celibate* (Seabury Press, 1974), p.53.
3. *The Sexual Celibate*, p.57.
4. Eileen Chandler, 'Educating Adolescent Girls', quoted in *The Church of England Newspaper*, 15 October 1982.
5. C.S. Lewis, *The Lion, the Witch and the Wardrobe* (Puffin, 1965), pp.147-149.

3
Pairing Off: Crime or Apprenticeship?

Ingrained in every human being is a thirst for emotional closeness with at least one other person. We examined this need in depth in chapter one. Inbuilt into most human beings is also a longing for closeness with a person of the opposite sex; the desire for the physical reunion which Adam and Eve rejoiced in when God created them for one another. We placed the spotlight on this need in chapter two and shall return to it in chapters five and six. Both needs, as we have seen, huddle under the overworked, umbrella term 'sexual intimacy'. Sexual intimacy in its widest sense includes emotional togetherness and bodily fusion.

But what has this to do with boy/girl relationships which might result in marriage, but which will almost certainly not do so? What is the purpose of such relationships? Are they dangerous time-wasters, dishonouring to the Lord, or do they have value for the Christian young person? If they do have value, should young Christians actively look for relationships with the opposite sex? And what about the 'If only I had a boyfriend (or girlfriend), everything would be all right' mentality? Is this foolish? Or does it contain a grain of truth? And how committed can such committed relationships be?

To these questions, and others like them, we apply ourselves in our quest for a foundation for firm, real and rich relationships. We will consider some of the implications involved in this chapter and the next.

Serious boy/girl relationships
Graham and Jane grew up in the same neighbourhood. Their parents knew one another well, they attended the same

church, and Graham and Jane shared the same interests: walking, cycling, badminton, music, missionary work in this country and overseas. For years they enjoyed a platonic friendship: going to church together, cycling for miles together, playing badminton most weeks. And they belonged to the same missionary prayer group.

Graham decided to apply for university in his home town instead of moving away, so they continued to see one another regularly during his undergraduate days. It was while he was studying for finals that his attitude to Jane changed. For no apparent reason he suddenly fell head-over-heels in love with her, and somehow needed to assure himself of her undying love for him.

To Jane's amazement, Graham blurted out a question one evening. 'Jane. I've got to know. Will you marry me?' Jane didn't know what to say. She liked Graham a lot. In many ways he was her best friend. But marriage! Why? She was pulling all the stops out working for her 'A' level examinations. Why think of marriage *now*? Yet she felt flattered too. 'Fancy someone proposing to me before I've even left school.'

The relationship changed gear after their conversation that night. For months, Jane deliberately avoided giving Graham an answer to his pressing question, but they started 'going out' in the sense that embracing and kissing crept into their friendship and escalated until heavy petting became a regular part of their diet. They dreamed dreams about the future, too. After Jane graduated they would settle down together, finish their training and then go off to serve God in India.

Jane departed for university confident of Graham's love and he of hers. They wrote long letters to each other at least twice a week. Graham would sometimes come to visit Jane in her hall of residence at weekends.

During her second term at university, Jane became strangely ill-at-ease about the relationship with Graham. She no longer looked forward to his visits. Somehow she sensed they were growing apart. They had little in common now, nothing to talk about. And yes, she could not deny that she was strongly attracted to a member of the Christian

Union in her college. Was she being unfaithful? Should she break off the relationship with Graham? But what reason should she give? And what of their long-term plans?

Graham sensed from her letters that Jane was changing but they did not talk at length about their disintegrating relationship until the Easter vacation. When Jane tried to explain, Graham became angry and defensive. He dared not show his hurt but rather exploded and accused her of being disloyal. His parents were hurt too. They had, by now, earmarked Jane as their son's bride-to-be. When they discovered Jane's uncertainty, they cut her dead. Neither they nor Graham ever spoke to Jane again. Even her own parents failed to understand her bewilderment. She eventually returned to university with some emotional bruises and batterings which she felt unable to voice to anyone. The experience also left her with several unanswered questions: Had the friendship been wrong in the first place? Had she and Graham been wrong to let romance colour their existing relationship? Had she been wrong to dream dreams about the future with Graham? Had she now been wrong to break it off?

What is the purpose of such friendships?
In responding to these imponderables the question needs to be asked: What is the purpose of these boy/girl friendships?

One of the purposes, as we saw in chapter one, is closeness, intimacy, the friendship which rejoices in discovering another person in life who is not only all for you, but who likes what you like; who is by your side, absorbed in exactly the same interests which add zest to your own life.

The richness of this kind of friendship is encapsulated on a card which stands on the desk in my study at the moment:

'A friend is a person who is for you always. . . . He wants nothing from you except that you be yourself. He is the one being with whom you can feel safe. With him you can utter your heart, its badness and its goodness. Like the shade of a great tree in the noonday heat is a friend. . . . He is the antidote to despair, the elixir of hope, the tonic for depression.' (Author anonymous)

At every stage of life, everyone needs another person with whom they experience the inexpressible comfort of this security; someone into whose heart they can pour their innermost hopes and fears, their disappointments and successes, someone who will listen and care and act appropriately.

In a moving, self-revealing poem entitled *Will you be my Friend?*, James Kavanaugh puts his finger on the heart of the situation: he shows that the need for such a friend is urgent:

Will you be my friend?
There are so many reasons why you never should;
I'm sometimes sullen, often shy, acutely sensitive,
My fear erupts as anger. I find it hard to give,
I talk about myself when I'm afraid
And often spend a day without anything to say.

But I will make you laugh
And love you quite a bit
And hold you when you're sad. . . .[1]

James Kavanaugh goes on to suggest that we need friends because there is a warm and tender side to each one of us which, though we hide it, yearns to express itself in the intimacy of friendship. So he repeats the question:

Will you be my friend?

A friend
Who far beyond the feebleness of any vow or tie
Will touch the secret place where I am really I. . . .

'The secret place where I am really I.' I love that phrase. In it lies the real reason for the craving that most people experience, the desire that someone in this world should discover and be concerned about the fearful, insecure and

vulnerable person who crouches behind the personality we
project to the watching world. So the poem persists:

And if at times I show my trembling side
(The anxious, fearful part I hide)

I wonder,
Will you be my friend?

Most of us long for an answer to that question, because the
need for friendship and love was ingrained in us deeply from
birth. We need someone to enter into the hidden places of our
hearts. We also need someone who asks us, 'Will you be *my*
friend?'

James Kavanaugh's quest is the quest of every man – and
of every woman – the urgent search for someone with whom
they can be real; someone with whom they can remove some
of their masks, but someone who will love them, respect and
understand them for who they really are underneath the
camouflage; someone who will 'touch the secret place where
I am really I'; but someone who will, in turn, open their heart
so that the friendship can be mutual.

We all need someone who will recognize the pain of our
personal vulnerability; someone who will, in turn, expose their
vulnerability. We all need someone who will seek to understand
our quota of defeats and tell us about theirs. We all need
someone who will pierce the layer of superficiality, understand
it for what it is: the pseudo-confidence which is a cover-up for
insecurity; someone who will admit, 'I identify with your pain
because I'm a wounded healer too.' We all need someone to
stay alongside us while we discover what maturity is all about;
someone who will permit us to stay alongside them while they
make similar discoveries.

We long for someone with whom we can feel safe, to whom
we can belong, to whom we can give ourselves to the fullest
extent of our being and who will similarly give of themselves in
return; someone who does not mind admitting that they love
with the 'L' plates on, that they have not yet learned all there is
to learn about this mystery called loving relationships.

Why other-sex friendships?

Adolescents and young adults frequently find that their parents and older people in the church have forgotten or never acquired the art of identifying with those who suffer the traumas of the between years: those who negotiate that frightening gulf which spans the dependency of childhood and the fully-fledged independence of adulthood. Peer-group friendships therefore flourish – quite rightly. Parents sometimes voice their alarm at the influence these friendships exert on their offspring. But surely most of us, in times of testing and trauma, turn for help to those who identify with our inner struggles, understand them, and offer us accepting love while we work through the pain?

James Kavanaugh is honest enough to lift the lid off his struggles; to ask that high-risk question: 'Will you be my friend?' What James Kavanaugh does not reveal is the need most people have, not simply for same-sex friendships, but for a soul-friend of the opposite sex. This need, as we have already seen in the earlier chapters of this book, is designed and implanted by God. It includes the need, on the male side, for the tenderness and trust which is communicated by women in a unique way, and the need, on the female side, for the respect, admiration, even flattery, which men give women and which increases their self-confidence and self-esteem. And, of course, it includes the need on both sides for touch. Touch adds spice to the warmth of togetherness. As one girl put it to me, describing an evening out with a boyfriend after several years of having no male contact, 'It felt so good to walk along the street holding hands with someone again: not just anyone – but *his* big, warm, supporting hand!'

Graham and Jane, whose friendship I sketched earlier, gave one another the support and acceptance, the love and understanding two maturing people need. Was their friendship a mistake, then, or could it be that, for a season, they enriched each other's lives, even helped one another to negotiate the wobbly stepping stones which seem to be the only route between childhood and adulthood? Was 'pairing off', in their case, so very wrong? Is 'pairing off', in fact, the Christian crime some make it out to be or is it, for some Christians, a necessary route to greater wholeness?

Pairing off: crime or necessity?

The Christian church, as often happens when people clamour for an answer to a question which is pertinent to them, remains sharply divided over the matter of boy/girl relationships. But at least three camps co-exist. Their varying emphases need to be weighed carefully by those searching for an answer to the pairing-off problem.

The first group is the prohibitionist camp. If you move in certain Christian circles, you will be warned against the dangers of romantic attachments at the adolescent and young adult stage of life. Young men will be advised to wait until they are 'thirty-ish' before they think of marriage. Young men and women will be encouraged to give their 'best years' to the Lord; not to be side-tracked by the trivia and encumbrances of boy/girl relationships with all the time wastage and heartbreak which such friendships frequently incur. Bible verses will be used to substantiate this teaching, notably 1 Corinthians 7:32–35, where Paul exhorts Christ's followers, 'I would like you to be free from concern. An unmarried man is concerned about the Lord's affairs – how he can please the Lord. But a married man is concerned about the affairs of this world – how he can please his wife – and his interests are divided. An unmarried woman or virgin is concerned about the Lord's affairs: her aim is to be devoted to the Lord in both body and spirit. But a married woman is concerned about the affairs of this world – how she can please her husband. I am saying this for your own good, not to restrict you, but that you may live in a right way in undivided devotion to the Lord.'

The prohibitionist argument

I know many, many Christians who are persuaded that this prohibitionist theory is biblical, and that Paul's word is the last word on the subject. Following Paul, or so they think, they abstain from one-to-one relationships with the opposite sex.

All I can say is that I admire them. The calibre of their Christian life knocks spots off many of their more liberally-minded counterparts. One has only to assess the harvest of their evangelistic zeal or survey the fruits of their Christian creativity to be deeply impressed by their productivity. In terms of sheer single-minded determination to serve Christ, their example is hard, if not impossible, to beat. I repeat, I admire them. Nevertheless, I question the wisdom of this prohibitionist dogma. I do so for several reasons.

First, we need to ask whether life is only about *achieving* for Christ. In the Martha and Mary conflict, Jesus seemed to emphasize man's need 'to be' as well as 'to do'. Yet many of these activists know little about 'being' before God. Even in prayer they have to achieve, it seems, and one possible explanation is that they have not yet learned how to be comfortable enough with themselves to be still with anyone, let alone God.

A second question needs to be asked: How are these young people to learn to tame the tiger of sex rampaging within and go on to integrate genital desires and loving relationships if they never encounter members of the opposite sex at close quarters? Many of the adherents of this teaching attended single-sex boarding schools. Many admit that they feel ill-at-ease in a one-to-one encounter with persons of the other sex. 'I admit I'm a prude. And I'm proud of it.' 'I just clam up when girls are around. I don't know what to say.' Many of the men camouflage this fear and embarrassment with a layer of seeming self-sufficiency which leaves the girls in their circle of acquaintances screaming in protest: 'Do you think these guys *really* don't need women or do they just pretend?'

Many of the women, too, conceal their very real pain and frustration. As one girl said to me as we discussed this book, 'Do say something about the "loneliness" of "waiting for the right guy". Speaking personally, I'm often found in floods of tears: tears of sheer frustration and insecurity. What's wrong with me? Why can't I catch one of these men?'

Consiously putting on a brave face through which to smile at the watching world, shrugging your shoulders with a philosophical, 'Oh well! I think I'll trog off to the library and concentrate on Finals', is one attitude. Repression is quite another. When I watch young people, influenced by this teaching, visibly shrink from members of the opposite sex, *repressing* sex rather than accepting it, it concerns me deeply.

It concerns me because such repression is harmful. It was not exemplified by Jesus, whom we are called to emulate. It results in stunted growth, not in Christian maturity. As I underlined in chapter two, we shall never be the outgoing, attractive, winning kind of person Jesus was until we have come to terms with our own sexuality, and this means rubbing shoulders (perhaps literally!) with members of the opposite sex.

I do not want to knock another man's deep convictions on this subject, but I do want to express my concern and to warn that this teaching does not hold water for everyone.

The third question which bothers me is this: Is it permissible to lift Bible verses from their context and make a theology of sex from them? In 1 Corinthians 7, Paul is not primarily addressing twentieth-century couples who are forced by circumstances to play the waiting game and who are therefore plagued with sexual hang-ups. No, Paul is addressing two separate sets of people who have each pestered him with specific requests: on the one hand the ascetics in Corinth were demanding that Paul should pontificate and pronounce celibacy as the only calling for Christian devotees, while on the other hand the more liberal converts wanted Paul's teaching to reflect their own contempt for celibacy and declare it irrelevant for Christ's followers.

Paul steers a middle course. Building on the teaching of Jesus which recognizes two vocations: marriage and singleness, to the former Paul says, 'You asked me if you should remain unmarried as a Christian. Well, it is certainly a most acceptable calling for a Christian. . . .But it is not an easy thing to remain single, and it's even more difficult in Corinth where you are surrounded by sexual immorality on every side. Therefore, it is probably best, in the first instance, that you should look to marriage as your calling.'[2] Having dampened their over-enthusiasm for celibacy, and having underlined the duty husbands and wives have to one another, he then sings the praises of celibacy and glories in his own vocation: single-minded service of Christ. But it is not often emphasized that in verse 7 of this chapter Paul underscores the fact that such celibacy is a special gift of the Holy Spirit, and he adds: 'Each has his own special gift from God, one of one kind and one of another.' Each must therefore discover his gift: abstention or involvement, and achieve his potential within his God-given calling.

The example of Jesus

We must, of course, base our behaviour on life-principles like the Pauline ones we have referred to, 'that you may live. . .in undivided devotion to the Lord' (1 Corinthians 7:35). The Christian, according to Paul, must live his life in the shadow of the Second Coming of Christ. Nothing must cramp his missionary style or dampen his missionary zeal.

But are we acting responsibly in taking one passage in isolation? Surely we must understand Paul's words in the context of what the New Testament teaches as a whole. As we saw at the end of chapter one of this book, Jesus' life-style was unique. On the one hand he was utterly devoted to his Father so that he could claim that even the words he spoke were given to him by God (John 12:50). On the other hand, this man Jesus, whose will was in complete alignment with his Father's, whose devotion to the Father never wavered, forged firm friendships across the sex barrier with all the risks that that entailed.

When I visited Israel the Gospel narratives came alive for me in a new way. As I attempted some of the walks that Jesus probably made regularly, I realized that he must have had a fine physique. The Gospels portray him as having a lively, logical mind, outstanding compassion, and a winning sense of humour. And he showed us how these superlative human characteristics could be channelled into serving God while at the same time relating closely to people of all ages and both sexes.

This leaves me with two serious question marks. First, is the prohibitionist theory following as nearly as possible in *Jesus'* footsteps? Second, is there a twin danger in this theory of 'elitism'; an encouragement to pour scorn on *God's* answer to loneliness: marriage? Neither of these views is biblical.

One further objection remains to be raised. Is it correct to assume that 'the best years' of our life are the young adult years? It is a well-known fact that a man reaches his peak in his forties, and that many women become more creative after the menopause than they were before. Surely the goal towards which we should travel at *every* stage of our life should be undivided loyalty to Christ?

The alternative: worldliness

It almost always happens that when one section of the church over-emphasizes teaching of the kind I have described, another section of the church over-reacts. This has happened with the strait-jacket teaching on boy/girl relationships which we have examined. 'What nonsense! Of course couples should pair off. Boys and girls need to learn from one another. Don't discourage them. Tell them that the taboos are a thing of the past. Touch is good and necessary. The important thing is to emphasize mutual love. "Love each other and do what you like." '

I am caricaturing. But this counter-attack which has been launched against the prohibitionist view is widely held today. Speaking personally, I am as unhappy about this view as the former one, for two reasons. First, because it is irresponsible. Second, because the focus has shifted from pleasing God to pleasing man and this, in my view, is of the essence of worldliness. One perplexed person wrote to me, 'So basically you have two opposing views but really everyone sits in the middle getting confused – except for those who've been drilled not even to think about it "till they're thirty!". . .I'm hoping you may be able to sort out the confusion or at least provide some kind of biblical framework to build on.'

An alternative

Is there an alternative? I believe there is. It is not an easy alternative. But then Jesus and Paul show us that neither marriage or singleness are easy options, so perhaps we should not expect the in-between stage to be free from problems either?

As Christians, we must learn to hold two things in tension: the constant readiness which is the outworking of our belief that Jesus could reappear at any moment – the kind of expectation which causes us to tingle with pure joy and anticipation at the very thought; and Jesus' solemn requirement that we must invest all that we have and all that we are in the here-and-now world (Matthew 25:14 ff.), giving glory to God by being fully alive. These two principles should govern our attitudes, our ambitions, our life-style, and all our relationships. 'If Jesus came back at this moment would I blush or leap for joy?' is a question which could punctuate our lives to advantage. It is a useful yardstick.

Apply this to the pairing-off problem and you come up with some interesting observations. We must not forget Paul's injunction to offer to God our undivided devotion, but neither must we assume that making warm relationships with a person of the opposite sex *need* distract us from serving Jesus any more than working for Finals does, or writing a book, or pursuing a time-consuming, expensive hobby like sailing or golf, or even accepting a responsible job, like the headship of a school or college. No-one suggests that we refuse to work or play to full capacity because the Lord might return at any moment. On the contrary, Christians believe that they will hear Jesus' heart-warming 'Well done, good and faithful servant', if they are found working responsibly and well when he returns.

Why isolate boy/girl relationships from these other potential distractions? Why not translate the principles which have relevance to every other area of life and apply them to this perplexing area? Why not re-evaluate by asking, 'Is there, in fact, value in such friendships even though they do not result in marriage?'

The value of one-to-one relationships

Donald Goergen, author of an important book on sexuality, *The Sexual Celibate*, is of the opinion, and I agree with him, that a woman becomes most truly a woman when she is loved and understood by a man. Similarly a man becomes most truly a man when a woman cares deeply for him. We are not talking here about 'pairing off', but deep friendships. It is as John Powell puts it, that each of us needs to be loved and cherished by persons of both sexes. Who we are and what we become depends largely on those who love us.[3]

During childhood, most of us were fortunate enough to experience unconditional love from our parents. When we are married, most of us are fortunate enough to rediscover this healing, unconditional love from our spouses. Could it be that the time-span between childhood and adulthood (when we are ready to accept the responsibilities of marriage or celibacy) might be considered our apprenticeship of love? Is it conceivable that one-to-one boy/girl relationships, if conducted sensibly, can contribute positively to the personal growth of the individual and even promote the process of sexual maturation? I am of the opinion that, even in the sex-saturated society in which we live, such phenomena can – and do – happen.

I sensed I saw it happen in the lives of two young friends of mine only recently. I shall call them Colin and Janet. They met at university. When Janet left home, she was disillusioned by Christianity, tired of being pressurized to seek the fullness of the Holy Spirit. Even so, at university she kept her own expression of her faith ticking over – just. Colin, on the other hand, found his feet spiritually at university. The pastor of the church he attended welcomed his gifts and made use of them. It was in this 'student church' that Colin and Janet met. Their friendship blossomed and gave birth to romantic love. They prayed together, relaxed together, went on holiday together, talked to one another about their hopes and ambitions, failures and insecurities. The basis of their relationship was a warm, accepting, understanding love: the desire to cherish the other, to draw out the other's potential.

After graduation, Colin and Janet continued to see one another spasmodically for several months. But Janet's training took her to far-flung parts of the world and Colin's to a remote part of England. Gradually, they grew apart. Since neither was ready for marriage and, in a sense, each had chosen singleness by opting for fulfilling, time-consuming careers, the demise of their romantic relationship was almost inevitable.

The parting of the ways was not without pain, but it was

not joyless either. As we asked, 'What have you learned from this relationship?', the list of benefits seemed endless. Colin discovered, among other things, that he had matured as a person, as a Christian, and as a man. Janet had looked up to him as the leader, and he had responded responsibly. He recognized that the self-centredness of adolescence (of which he was now mildly ashamed) had been replaced by 'other awareness' (not just 'Janet-awareness' but a deeper understanding of the needs of others in general). Selfishness had been dislodged by outgoingness and compassion and much of the gaucherie born of teenage insecurity had been banished, to be replaced by gentleness and tenderness.

Janet, too, realized that the friendship had contributed to her spiritual growth. In partnership with Colin she had rediscovered the delight of serving God: running holiday clubs for children, using her musical gifts, leading 'welcome' campaigns for overseas students. Listening to Colin's male insights had broadened her own view of God and helped her to understand the relevance of the Holy Spirit to her own life.

In addition, friendship with Colin taught her how to relate to members of the opposite sex; how to feel comfortable in their presence. She realized that one of the riches Colin had given her was the ability to accept her own femininity. indeed, her ability to view herself as God and others viewed her had escalated because of this friendship. And as Janet had relaxed as a person, fun bubbled out of her, she learned to be gentle rather than brittle. Her self-confidence had not only taken root; it had grown.

Colin and Janet will never marry. That does not invalidate their relationship, in my view. God used it. The personal legacy each is left with enriches their lives today. Moreover, look at *how* God used it: to transform both of them more into his own likeness. We have used words like compassion, gentleness, tenderness, delight in pleasing God, to describe the changes which took place. These are words we would use to describe the earthly life and ministry of Jesus too. These two certainly made mistakes in their loving of one another and they would be the first to admit it. Even so, they strug-

gled to hold these two things in tension: God's sovereignty
and responsible loving.

The new need

The new and urgent need is not that restrictive word 'Don't'
but rather education. My generation has a responsibility to
the younger generation to teach them *how* to make serving
God their goal while not amputating or repressing their God-
given desire for one-to-one closeness.

But the going is tough, as I implied at the beginning of this
section. You must decide for yourself whether the risks of
pairing off are worth taking, or whether total abstinence
would be more profitable for you spiritually, emotionally,
socially. You must decide whether the legacy left by a friendship of the Colin-Janet variety or the Graham-Gill variety is
equal in value or of parallel value to the harvest reaped for
Christ by those who try to live out-and-out for him, in the
sense that any emotional entanglement with the opposite sex
is taboo. The crunch question to pose in balancing one
against the other is: 'What pleases God?' Is it winning souls
for Christ? Is it dedicating all you have and are in the service
of the King of kings and Lord of lords? Or is it being
personally transformed into the likeness of Christ by having
your rough edges sandpapered in the love and tumble of
human relationships? Could it be that all three are necessary
and that our near-impossible task at every stage of adolescence and adulthood is to find the tight-rope *and* keep our
balance?

'Yes! But you don't have to "pair off" to have your corners
knocked off.' A young man, accusing me of worldliness,
made this angry protest after I'd spoken at a Christian
Union meeting on one occasion. No. That is perfectly true.
Yet surely everyone would admit that the apprenticeship of
love served in these special one-to-one boy/girl relationships
introduces a new taste to life? These friendships are not the
same as same-sex friendships, sibling relationships or the
fellowship which enriches the lives of those fortunate enough
to have 'brothers and sisters' in Christ. They are deliciously
different. Whether they distract you from your number one

mission in life, to 'seek first the kingdom of God and his righteousness', depends on how you conduct them. The 'how to' of conducting responsible and enriching relationships is the subject we must tease out in the next chapter.

Notes for chapter three

1. James Kavanaugh, quoted by Jim Bigelow in *Love Has Come Again* (Lakeland, 1978), p.47.
2. David Gillett's paraphrase in *A Place in the Family* (Grove Pastoral Series 6, 1981), p.8.
3. See John Powell, *The Secret of Staying in Love* (Argus, 1974).

4
Radical Relationships

'Pairing off is one of the major problems in the church here. We lose more young Christians from the church because of boy/girl relationships than through any other one contributing cause. Couples fall in love, they form an exclusive relationship, they hive off into a corner, backslide from the faith and before long they've slipped out of the fellowship altogether.'

The person who made that statement to me was a youth worker. Our conversation highlighted two pressing needs: first, the urgent need to define this over-used phrase 'pairing off'; second, the need to educate Christian couples in the 'how to' of radical one-to-one relationships. If God, architect of our bodies, spirits, and emotional and psychological make-up, created us, as he did, lonely in the absence of a person of the opposite sex, it is inconceivable that such relationships automatically push us into spiritual apathy. The fault, if God dreamed up the design, cannot be with the design itself. Perhaps we have failed to read the Maker's instructions?

In this chapter, then, we define 'pairing off'. We go on to examine some of the questions left dangling in mid-air from the last chapter. And we consider some new problems. How do you find such friendships? Do they just happen, like catching chicken-pox, do they come through fervent prayer, or as divine favours for pious people, or do you go out and search diligently for them, like the woman looking for her lost coin? If you are fortunate enough to find such a potential friendship, how do you get started? How do you say 'No' if a particular friendship seems wrong? Are there dangers to avoid? If so, what are they?

Pairing off

'Pairing off' is frequently used in a derogatory way to describe an exclusive, possessive, even gruesome twosome: the kind of couple who cut themselves off from others and the maelstrom of life, spend a great deal of time shut up in their room or car, resent the visits of friends which are seen as 'intrusions' and rely heavily on petting and the sexual thrills they give each other through caressing. The dictionary seems to support this common usage. Of 'pair', it writes: thing with two similar parts not used apart (p. of scissors, trousers); mated couple; pair off: divide entirely into pairs.

But 'pairing off' can be used in a mildly teasing, twinkle-in-the-eye, warm-tone-of-voice, way. Here it describes a one-to-one relationship between a boy and a girl who are powerfully attracted to one another, who are learning to be special to one another, and who feel they belong to one another, however temporary that 'belongingness' may prove to be. It has that 'everyone loves a lover' seal of approval.

As we took trouble to note in the last chapter, partnerships which fall into the second category can contribute to our emotional and spiritual growth. They can hinder it too, of course; so much depends on how they are conducted. But relationships which fit the niche of my first definition of pairing off should, in my view, find no place in the life of the committed Christian. These friendships quickly become claustrophobic, inward-turned, time-wasting and un-healthy. Sticky and greedy as it is, the relationship quickly stagnates. Even so the couple refuses either to separate or change its behaviour-pattern. They continue to make demands of the other, continue to ignore others, continue to neglect their responsibilities and deliberately reject opportunities to serve Christ and to mature as people. Such worldly wastage of young life is tragic.

As we have observed before, the realm of relationships, as indeed every other area of our lives, must be lived in the consciousness that King Jesus could return at any time. We must constantly apply that touchstone of behaviour we've applied before: 'Supposing Jesus returned *now?* What would he, the Master, think of our life-style?'

The problem is that most of us convince ourselves that Jesus will not come tonight nor even within the next five years and so we carry on, careless and complacent. But if we are serious about our Christian commitment, dare we watch the years roll by and continue leading mediocre Christian lives? Metropolitan Anthony Bloom thinks not. Prayer and commitment to Christ, he claims, bring new responsibilities:

> We must learn to behave in the presence of the invisible Lord as we would in the presence of the Lord made visible to us. This implies primarily an attitude of mind and then its reflection upon the body. If Christ was here, before us, and we stood completely transparent to his gaze, in mind as well as in body, we would feel reverence, the fear of God, adoration, or else perhaps terror but *we should not be so easy in our behaviour as we are.*[1]

Add to this apt challenge a solemn question of Jesus: ' "Why do you call me 'Lord, Lord,' and not do what I tell you?" ' (Luke 6:46), and perhaps I need not put the screws on any more.

If you recognize yourself from my description, if you have been sucked into an exclusive, emotion-draining relationship, you have not committed the unforgivable sin but you have been unwise. Don't wallow in guilt or self-pity. Admit your failure. Confess the sickliness of it to God. Repent; that is, determine to live differently. Perhaps go with your partner and talk to someone who can point you in the direction of Jesus' style of one-to-one relationships. Or, read on!

One-to-one relationships
When that delicious thing we call pairing off happens to us, it does not discharge us from that basic code of Christian conduct summed up by Jesus in Matthew 22:37: 'Love the Lord your God with all your heart and with all your soul and

with all your mind. . . .Love your neighbour as yourself.'
Love in this context does not mean sentimentality, gushing
feelings; it does mean love in action. Service. Self-sacrifice.
So, how do we hold these two things in tension: our earnest
desire to please God and the sometimes more urgently felt
heart-longing for intimacy?

We shall return to this question later in this chapter. First I
want to reflect on the difference between the kind of relationship I have ruled out of court and the kind I am advocating.

Lewis Smedes captures the subtle nuances of healthy relationships across the sex barrier in this way:

> Whenever a man and woman relate to each other as
> persons it adds an indefinable tinge of adventure and
> excitement, uncertainty and curiosity to the relationship.
> It colors the conversation with all sorts of brighter and
> lighter hues absent from the paler conversations between
> members of the same sex. The sexual dimensions of a
> totally 'innocent' relationship provide the added adven-
> ture and mystery of personal relationships that unisex
> society would sadly lack. . . .We should be conscious of it,
> accept it and rejoice in it. The more we affirm it with
> thanks, the less likely we are to be deluded by the fear that
> any sexually exciting relationship will lead to the
> bedroom.[2]

Compare the language used to describe these relationships:
'adventure', 'mystery', 'colour', 'excitement', with the words
I used to sum up the in-grown kind of friendship: 'claustrophobic', 'emotion-draining', 'inward-turned'. One kind is
selfish and causes couples to shrivel. The other kind puts a
spring in your step, a twinkle in your eye and a song in your
heart. As a friend of mine once put it, healthy relationships
make you glow all over and feel warm inside.

Even though a person may never have embarked on a
close relationship of the kind we envisage, they sense the
cosiness, the contentment, the thrill and the euphoria such
relationships bring. 'I see couples strolling along the river-
bank hand in hand or laughing into each other's eyes or

sitting in the park together and I want what they've got even though I don't know what "it" really is.' 'It' somehow communicates itself through a wink, a knowing look, a laugh, a touch or that intangible something we now call 'vibes'. But the vibes are good. Most want what these couples have because this love does not stagnate, it overflows. Everyone feels the benefit of its energy. That, of course, prompts a question: How do these friendships start?

Finding friendships

How *do* such friendships spring to life? One moment they're not there; the next minute they're flourishing. How do they happen? Do you pray for them, search for them, wait for them, manipulate them? Or what?

Many Christians I know *do* seek for romantic relationships. The inner longing is so great when that broody feeling sweeps over you that this is perfectly understandable. It is understandable, but, I suggest, counter-productive, time-wasting and unwise. As we noted in the last chapter, our first aim, as Christians, is to seek the kingdom of God; to serve the King. If we attend this meeting and that conference, this houseparty and that camp in the expectation of finding an eligible partner, or if we spend hours agonizing in prayer for a romantic relationship, we may well end up frustrated, disillusioned, embittered and spiritually impoverished because we have become absorbed with self, even wallowed in self-pity. We shall have steered our boat off course, therefore. What is more, unless we are very careful, the cattle-market mentality creeps into our thinking and governs it. As one girl expressed it to me, after her first few Christian Union meetings: 'I now know what it must feel like to be in the arena on market day. As a group of girls came into the meeting you could almost feel certain blokes eyeing you up and down. It was horrible.' This girl happened to attend a university where there were fewer women than men. But the same principle applies in many colleges and in any church which attracts crowds of eligible single young people. Girls are not guiltless: they have their own methods of short-listing certain eligible bachelors. Instead of finger-pointing, if we are serious about our commitment to Christ we will ask the Holy Spirit to deliver us from this snare and renew our mind continuously so that we meet fellow Christians as brothers and sisters in Christ, not as potential lovers or sex conquests.

So how *do* such friendships seed themselves? The most fertile soil is to be found in an unexpected field: in Christian service, creativity groups and fellowship groups.

Talk to any happily married Christian couple, ask them how they met, and it becomes clear that God is no man's debtor. We cannot outgive his generosity. The story repeats itself over and over again with delightful regularity and a complete lack of monotony: two single people run a youth club or Christian organization together and friendship flourishes as they strive for Christ side by side. Friendship thrives and blossoms into marriageable love. Or a couple might find themselves involved in a shared-interest activity: music, rambling, drama, sport. The experiences encountered on the way will be varied: shared joy, shared effort, shared fulfilment, shared tension, shared festivities. This variety of sharing often provides the place where deeper sharing, deeper friendships, 'in-loveness' are conceived. The two people concerned never joined the club or offered their talents with the intention of finding a partner. They were simply expressing their God-given creativity or using their skills for Christ. In fact, if they had deliberately sought romance it would probably have eluded them. Yet while they absorbed themselves in other activities, that elusive but welcome guest, an attraction for a person of the opposite sex, took up residence.

It reminds me of springtime in the country. You see the trees weighed down with blossom, you watch the rhododendron buds unfold and you wait for that other sign of spring: the call of the first cuckoo. Look for the cuckoo and you will rarely find it. But work in your garden or go for a ramble and, sure enough, in the fullness of his time, that cheeky cuckoo-call will echo through the valley. And you rejoice because summer, too, is almost here.

Getting going

'But how do we get going? The brothers in our fellowship seem so slow.' When I toured Singapore and Malaysia, girls clamoured for a solution to this tiresome question. (In Malaysia and Singapore the Christians have a delightful custom of calling one another 'brother' and 'sister'.) But the problem is not simply Singaporean or Malaysian. English girls pose the same problem rather more crudely, 'How *do* you catch a Christian man?'

I well understand the frustration girls feel (after all, I am feminine too), but it is useless to fume. Perhaps we females need to understand the problem from the male point of view?

Rightly or wrongly, the initiative still rests with the man. Most girls prefer the men to do the chasing. Most men prefer to make the first move in relationships even in these liberated days. Thus, all the onus rests on the men. But as some inexperienced, would-be 'suitors' have explained to me, 'It's all right for the girl. If we make the first move, she can assume that we like her, otherwise we wouldn't have invited her out in the first place. But if we take the plunge, how do we know she won't turn us down? Supposing I make a fool of myself? Supposing I *think* a girl likes me a lot, but all the time I've been kidding myself? And worse, supposing I ask her out and she gets more serious than I want to be at this stage of my life? It's such a precarious business. At times I'm plain scared. And what *do* you talk about on that first date?'

Comments like these remind me of James Kavanaugh's admission in the poem 'Will you be my friend?' which I quoted in the last chapter: 'I'm sometimes sullen, often shy, acutely sensitive.' Many men are like that, though few admit it, since the fashion is to imitate macho man. And, of course, not all men dither. Some enjoy the 'Does she or doesn't she like me?' phase and soon pluck up courage to discover the truth of the situation for themselves.

But since many men do confess to shyness and vulnerability it adds weight to what we have already said about the value of group friendships, shared activities; of young people enjoying being alongside each other united by an activity outside of themselves. If a young man in the church music group forms a close friendship with one of the girls, it can be the most natural thing in the world to invite her out for coffee or a pizza after the practice. No mention need be made of 'going out' at first. If they enjoy one another's company and the attraction is mutual, this will become self-evident and they will continue to meet in the context of the group and outside it. If the man is uncertain after several attempts at decoding the girl's reaction to him, he could perhaps arrange a foursome or sixsome in an attempt to get to know the girl better. If the friendship is true friendship, it will include the ability to communicate not just facts but feelings, and the couple will find that they can talk about their feelings for one another without the man ever having to make a formal proposal, 'Will you go out with me?'

Saying 'No'

I am writing this in a cottage in the country. It's dark outside and a moth, attracted by the light of my angle-poise lamp, is pressing against the window-pane near my desk, clearly frustrated that the invisible barrier blocks his flight. The waiting game sets many a girl into a similar state of agitation. Even so, we owe it to the men in the fellowship to understand them. If we put ourselves in their shoes and begin to appreciate their vulnerability, we shall take great care not to hurt them unnecessarily if they do decide to make the first move and we decide that this friendship is not right at this moment in time, or with this person. In such an eventuality, our 'No' must be clear but kind; firm but gentle. And we should never stoop to gossiping about the person who approached us behind his back, or making up a string of excuses or avoiding him. Such bullets, once fired, not only wound, they scar.

Of course, the young man may well be disappointed. That cannot be avoided. What can be avoided is any unnecessary trampling over his feelings with offhandedness, mockery, rudeness, or bluntness. Although they do not always admit it as readily as women, men have feelings too and are easily hurt.

A few do's

But your reply may not be a regretful 'No'. It might be a grateful 'Yes'. Whether this is the long-awaited invitation or whether it comes as a bolt from the blue, there are certain do's and don'ts which Christians serious about their commitment to Christ should observe. We now look at these one by one in an attempt to return to the question I left unanswered earlier, 'How does Jesus show us how to relate?'; in an attempt, too, to ensure that such friendships do not lead you into a spiritual deep-freeze or on to an emotional scrap-heap but rather make a lasting contribution to your spiritual, emotional and sexual growth.

The first 'do' that needs to be underlined several times is this: Do remember that we are vulnerable. A friend of mine once captured the subtleties of this vulnerability in a line-drawing which emerged from a doodle. With his permission, I have reproduced it here because it speaks more powerfully than words.

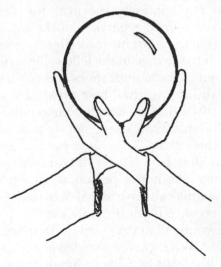

We are vulnerable . . .

In the kind of relationship which we are envisaging, the sphere, the relationship, is as fragile as a bird's egg. If either party removes their hand, the egg crashes to the ground, cracks or breaks: the contents spill. Similarly if either or both partners grasp the egg in a possessive, jealous gesture, they will crack it and again the relationship will be damaged.

At the moment, where I live, my neighbours and I keep finding little blue eggshells in our gardens. 'It's the magpies,' my knowledgeable neighbour told me the other day. 'They steal the starling's eggs and eat them, then litter the ground with the broken eggshells.'

The society in which we live today is not unlike that. It, too, is littered with the fractured remains of once-promising relationships as well as the wastage and spoil of cheap and trivialized relationships. In certain circles casual relationships are encouraged, even applauded. But this is worldliness at its worst: living for self, living for kicks, treating people whose lives are precious to God as toys. Such worldliness, like a creeping sickness, is infiltrating Christian circles causing a frightening malaise among young people today. If we are to be true to ourselves, to the Lord whom we have enthroned as King of our lives, and to our brothers and sisters in Christ who are every bit as fragile as we ourselves are, and if we are to create Jesus' kind of relationships, we must keep this 'we are vulnerable' slogan ever before us. We must learn to tread as gently in our relationships as Jesus did. In John 13–17 it becomes apparent that loving the way Jesus did includes a desire to protect the loved one from unnecessary hurt; it reflects, too, the fact that Jesus assumed responsibility for others' feelings. This attitude, not the antithesis, self-gratification at all costs, should characterize our one-to-one relationships.

Watch your thought-life
In practice this means, among other things, watching your thought-life. Our imagination, when dedicated to God, is one of the most powerful senses entrusted to us. With it, we can be transported in worship; with it we can live, for a while, in a world a plane above the tragedies and traumas of this life; with it we can write poignant poems or be inspired to paint pictures that 'speak'. But the imagination is equally capable of disrupting our lives, of upsetting our equilibrium completely.

If you have ever fallen head-over-heels in love you will know exactly what I mean. The infatuation leaves no part of

you untouched. Your mind spins as thoughts of the beloved
swirl round vying for attention. The whole of your body
tingles at the thought of the beloved's touch or loving look.
Your will melts like butter in the sun. And your imagination
runs riot, untiringly embroidering what has been: every
cherished glance and word and embrace; feeding on all that
the relationship is or seems to be and over-glamourizing
what will be. You may push these thoughts away, but like a
jack-in-the-box they pop up again, dance before your eyes,
mesmerize you as they clamour for attention.

Such infatuation can be fun for a while, but the accompanying fantasies can be fatal. Your imagination roams out
of bounds. You protest that you cannot call it to heel. But
that is not Jesus' verdict. Christ-like friendships recoil from
lustful daydreams (Matthew 5:28). As Martin Luther
shrewdly observed, using a different metaphor, 'You can't
stop birds flying over your head but you can stop them
nesting in your hair.'

Recognize the difference between infatuation and affection
We not only can – we must. Unless we do stop these birds
nesting in our hair we shall put the relationship in jeopardy.
Fantasies, like seeds hidden in the warm soil of the desert,
germinate fast and produce prolific growth. Just as seasonal
rains will transform the desert into a garden within hours so
fantasies, if nourished, will take root and proliferate. The
problem then is that you manipulate the relationship to take
up where your fantasies left off, thus refusing it permission to
develop at its own, more innocent, pace.

This leads me to my next 'do'. Remember that infatuation,
overwhelming as it is, fun as it is, has little to do with
affection. Infatuation, in fact, is usually thoroughly 'me-
centred' rather than 'other-centred'. You fall for someone,
you beguile yourself into believing yourself deeply in love
with this person round whom your dreams revolve, you
believe yourself ready to renounce your absorption with self
for the sake of the well-being of this other person. Then, one
morning, you wake up to discover that the euphoria has
evaporated in the night. What is more, you find yourself held

captive by identical feelings for *another* person.

Jesus, attractive as he was, in all probability attracted female infatuations and fantasies, though no doubt he was able to discourage them without hurting the persons concerned. But, as we observed in chapter one, he was prayerfully selective about the close relationships he encouraged. And if we are wise, we shall follow his example even in the climate in which we live; even when the peer-group pressure to pair off is fierce.

Possessiveness

Another 'do' which is essential in any one-to-one friendship is this: beware of the booby-trap bombs of possessiveness and jealousy. I sometimes find myself aching for couples where the girls act rather like the rhododendron roots I saw strangling some pine trees on one occasion. These girls climb and cling and refuse to let go. I agonize, too, for couples where either partner is consumed with jealousy every time their partner enjoys the companionship of another member of the opposite sex.

One young man was honest enough to express this problem to me recently. 'The jealousy inside me is terrible. It makes me want to possess her. I want her to walk with me to church. I want her to sit next to me. I want us to do everything together: little things like washing and shopping; big things like studying.'

In answer to my question, 'How do you feel about these demands?', his girlfriend pulled a face and admitted that this possessiveness was fast feeling claustrophobic. 'It feels more committed than I'm prepared to be at this stage. It's not that I don't love him. It's just that I don't want to act like his wife until we are married.'

That puts the situation in a nutshell. A relationship where jealousy and possessiveness prevail inevitably becomes claustrophobic. People suffering from claustrophobia look for an escape-route. They fear that unless they escape they will choke. In Jesus' style of friendships there is an absence of such strangulation. Far from stifling his friends, Jesus encouraged them, as we saw in chapter one, to love each

other, to express this affection, to discover their God-
ordained mission and to be caught up in it. Jesus provided
his friends with the free and fearless space to grow as individuals and in the service of God.

Promote your partner's growth

And one of the purposes of love, on the pattern of Jesus, is
actively to promote the growth of the loved one. This is the
key to radical one-to-one relationships. They do not exist for
self-gratification or sexual thrills, but to provide the environment where each friend can be loved into the next phase of
personal growth.

Look at it this way. Good parents bring a child into the
world, not to feed their own need to be needed, but to
unpack, with the growing child, God's purposes for this new
life. Indeed, the chief purpose of parenthood is to provide the
environment where the little person can discover his God-
given potential. Similarly, one of the purposes of marriage is
to take up where parents left off. In healthy Christian marriages, each partner encourages the other to plumb the
depths of their God-given love.

One-to-one relationships, as I see them, are the bridge
which spans the gulf between parental love and marital love.
Even though a particular boy/girl friendship may never
result in marriage, its main aim should coincide with the
relationships which precede and follow it: to generate the
atmosphere where the loved one's further growth can most
easily take place.

True love never restricts or hinders a person's growth. On
the contrary, as Jesus demonstrated here on earth, true love
gives the loved one roots, by providing a secure place of
belonging, but it also gives the loved one wings, permission
to come and go as he pleases.

If we keep this high purpose of one-to-one loving before us,
the Christian church need not bewail the pairing off problem
I mentioned at the beginning of this chapter, but will rather
rejoice in the maturity and zeal of the young people who
serve the King.

A few don'ts

Don't, then, trap each other or deprive one another of the joy of serving God. If your boyfriend is endowed musically, set him free, no, encourage him to join the music group in church. Yes. This will be costly for you. You will appear to your friends to be statusless because you sit alone. You will be denied the physical cosiness of sharing your songsheet with him and maybe brushing his hand as you do so. But think of the benefits for your boyfriend (see Matthew 5:14ff.), think of the value of his ministry within the body of Christ, look at the situation from God's perspective. Chew over the example of Jesus. Ask him to purge you of the resentment that *would* restrict your partner's movements.

Don't over-commit yourself

Many couples who start going out in their middle or late teens feel very committed to one another, like Graham and Jane whose relationship I described in chapter three. A certain amount of commitment is clearly important. But don't *over*-commit yourself as they did, planning for years ahead when both of them would change in the intervening years. No. If, one day, engagement and marriage are right for this relationship, that is the time to make long-lasting promises and plans. Not now. One of the vital lessons Jesus taught us is to live one day at a time, to live it to the full, and to live it for God. If Graham and Jane and Graham's parents had lived life as Jesus lived it, Graham and Jane could have parted without bitterness and without deliberately inflicted wounds.

Don't precipitate a teenage marriage

And don't let infatuation or euphoria or pressure from family or friends precipitate a youthful marriage. The statistics suggest that 50% of teenage marriages result in divorce within the first five years. These figures are frightening. Young adulthood is a time of change. Enjoy the richness of one-to-one relationships by all means, but be prepared to wait for the responsibilities of marriage.

And, as I implied at the beginning of this chapter, don't

allow this relationship to fritter away God's gift of time. Don't reject opportunities for serving God. Don't cut yourselves off from others. They need you and you need them.

Much of what I have written goes against the world's grain (and we haven't tackled the petting problem yet). If you set out to forge Jesus' style of friendships you will be swimming against society's tide. You may be mocked, you may be rejected, you may feel foolish.

But Christianity never did pretend to pander to worldly opinions. Neither did it ever pretend to be for the chicken-hearted. No. Christ turns worldly standards on their heads and calls us to live differently. To live differently means to stick out like a sore thumb. It means you have to be tough. It involves a radical re-appraisal of much we take for granted. It calls for radical relationships.

I don't guarantee you an easy ride. But what will happen if you live life as Jesus lived it is that any relationships you make will leave you with few regrets, few blushes and, instead of a nasty taste in your mouth, a grateful prayer: 'Lord, for what we have each received from you in this relationship, make us eternally grateful.' What is more, if you ever do marry, you will never be embarrassed to introduce your spouse to an 'old flame'. Such walking in the light is liberty.

Notes for chapter four

1. Anthony Bloom, *Living Prayer* (Libra, 1976), p.12 (italics mine).
2. Lewis Smedes, *Sex in the Real World* (Lion, 1976), p.96.

5
Sex before Marriage

The purpose of one-to-one relationships for the Christian, as we saw in chapter three, is not primarily to provide partners with a series of sex jaunts but rather to promote the emotional and spiritual growth of both people. Such partnerships, sandwiched as they are between the intimacy once provided by parental love and the intimacy of the hoped-for marriage relationship, are gap fillers. Such gap fillers can be valuable. If each partner provides the other with the sympathetic care every young person needs during the maturing years, if the essential ingredients of tenderness, understanding and solidarity with the peculiar pains of the growing years are present, the relationship could be one of those rich friendships for which we thank God, which we look back on and recognize that, within the love of God, have made us real.

By real, I mean genuine, less afraid to remove the masks behind which most of us hide, authentic, Christ-like. But, as the velveteen rabbit in Margery Williams' touching children's story reminds us, such 'realness' takes a very long time to mature:

'What is REAL?' asked the Rabbit one day when he and his close friend the Skin Horse were lying side by side near the nursery fender. 'Does it mean having things that buzz inside you and a stick-out handle?'

'Real isn't how you are made,' said the Skin Horse. 'It's a thing that happens to you. When a child loves you for a long, long time, not just to play with, but REALLY loves you, then you become Real.'. . .

'Does it happen all at once, like being wound up. . .or bit by bit?'

'It doesn't happen all at once,' said the Skin Horse. 'You become. It takes a long time. . . .Generally, by the time you are Real, most of your hair has been loved off, and your eyes drop out and you get loose in the joints and very shabby. But these things don't matter at all, because once you are Real you can't be ugly, except to people who don't understand.'[1]

If you want to discover how the Rabbit became real you have to read the book for yourself. And it's well worth buying because the Skin Horse is very wise and extremely accurate. Real is not how we were first made. It implies growth and maturing. We become real through the patience of those who love us. And most young people, even those who are not Christians, admit that in close one-to-one relationships, what they most want is this depth of understanding, this caring from someone else, which will give them permission to be real with at least one other person in this brash and uncertain world.

But herein lies a problem. These one-to-one relationships, as I have said, bridge the gulf between parent-child intimacy and the intimacies of marriage. But in parent-child loving, cuddling, kissing, caressing are all natural, necessary and right. Similarly, in the marital relationship, the intimacies of touch lie at the core of the friendship. They are an essential and integral part of the relationship. And the *desire* to express love by touching does not evaporate during the in-between years. It accelerates. So what are young couples supposed to do with the touch bomb? How do they resolve the petting problem?

This is the subject which we must now bring to the forefront of our minds. In the next two chapters, then, we shall be handling such hot potatoes as these: 'Is it all right for two people who really love each other to sleep together? If not, where should we draw the petting line? Isn't the Bible's teaching rather out-moded and unreasonable, even unrealistic? Doesn't it turn the so-called God of love into a spoil-sport? How on earth *do* you cool the sex urge? And what happens if you fail?'

Many sincere Bible-believing Christians clamour for an answer to questions like these, like the girl who wrote to me on one occasion:

'I am 18 and became a Christian six months ago. I have been going out with my boyfriend for over a year now and we make love together. I've never really thought about it being wrong or right until just recently and it's causing me a lot of problems.

'On one side I've got parents who forbid it. On the other side I've got friends who think it's perfectly acceptable. Then I've got God telling us it's wrong, and I really don't understand why it's wrong. Of course, I understand why it's wrong for some people but my boyfriend and I have such a great relationship. It's very hard for my boyfriend suddenly to hear from me that we no longer can have that side of a relationship. Surely there's room in the Christian faith to make your own decisions about things? Anyway, I find I'm rebelling against God because I just don't understand some of the Christian principles. It's important for me to be clear about my faith. I would be so grateful if you could write back to me.'

I admired that girl for writing as she did. I know that it was costly to do so. I want to use her letter as a basis for discussion.

Spoil-sport God?

The first thing to understand is that God is not a sugar-daddy giving his children everything they want exactly when they want it. Nor is he a spoil-sport, sitting in the heavenly places, waiting for the precise moment when we are about to enjoy ourselves and choosing that moment to thunder an almighty 'Don't' from heaven. No. God is love. Love: self-lessness, goodness, the desire to give us only the best, is what God is. Love is the essence of his being.

Even so there are Christians who nurse the dread that God is a killjoy. When they seek for guidance about anything they think of the thing they least want to do and decide that that must be God's will. This killjoy God is a figment of men's imagination, born of neurosis and bad teaching. He is not the God of the Bible. Similarly, the spoil-sport God is the picture of God painted for us by Satan way back in Genesis 3, a picture which will be finally phased out when we see Jesus face to face, and which could be phased out now if we would focus on the Jesus of the Gospels. But, of course, Satan redirects our attention from Jesus to Satan's lies. So a paraphrase of Genesis 3:1 and Genesis 3:4 for the purposes of our study, might read rather like this: 'What a terrible, selfish God, God is. Has he told you to avoid pre-marital genital intercourse? Fancy! What a wet blanket he is. Has he told you this will soil your soul or harm you? What nonsense! Far from being harmed, you will become an adult. By losing your virginity you will become a skilled lover, a VIP.'

This subtle, lying, persuasive whisper sounds so much more attractive to the young Christian than swimming against a sex-crazy tide, that too often they swallow the lie, behave promiscuously and then rail at God because this behaviour cuts them off from him.

Sex and the media

The media reinforce this lie. A certain newspaper once published a series of articles which made these claims: 'These days there's nothing wrong if a girl wants to go to bed with a guy'; 'I'm a *BIG* girl now – I'm going to stop worrying about what my mother told me and enjoy this wonderful moment' (of sexual promiscuity). The same newspaper published articles by mothers *advising* their teenagers to sleep around.

Or I think of the film *Endless Love,* the story of the sexual awakening of a seventeen-year-old boy and a sixteen-year-old girl; of their total obsession with each other. The director said of the controversy surrounding that film: 'I'm not encouraging fifteen-year-olds to make love. They do that anyway. I'm just telling them it's quite normal.'

Or, again, I think of a recently published book aimed to bring twelve- to sixteen-year-olds into an awareness of their sexual responsibilities. The author records the reactions of certain teenagers in this age-bracket to the loss of their virginity. 'The loss of virginity has an enormous effect on boys and girls. . . .Boys have mainly positive feelings. You feel that you have matured, you're proud of yourself and feel a sense of accomplishment. You feel like a man and it's something to boast about. You feel you've conquered something, and are relieved that you can finally tell the truth if someone asks you if you're still a virgin.

'Girls too have positive feelings. You're a woman. You feel fully-fledged and confident. You feel relief that you've crossed a hurdle and will now be accepted by your friends as grown up. . . .You've joined the adult world. You're a VIP.'[2]

My heart bled as I copied out that quotation. What Satan hides, and what the author of this book fails to point out, is the underlying reason for these so-called 'positive' feelings: that this is pandering to the conformist in us all I described in an earlier chapter, that this is yielding to group pressure, that such bragging about sexual conquests is the price you pay for acceptance in certain teenager and young adult circles. What remains concealed is the fact that these positive feelings are often transient: they turn to the lasting guilt we shall examine later, they become the skeletons in the cupboard whose presence haunts us unbearably. What remains concealed is the fact that sexual intimacies, forced, indeed inflicted is not too strong a word, on girls in their teens leave behind a trail of scarred memories, a fear of sex within marriage, a distaste, even disgust, for one of God's most precious gifts. What remains concealed is that this is not God's superlative gift of genital fusion but a tawdry substitute, sex trivialized.

As we shall go on to observe, God wants to preserve us from this sick substitute for sex. God would protect us from the confusion and the pain and the unhealed, tormenting memories. He says what he says because Love is what he is and love wants to protect the loved one from unnecessary hurt. God is no spoil-sport. Through-and-through Love is what he is.

God and sex
So what *does* God say about sex? As we saw in chapter two,

our God is pro-sex. You will find nothing negative in the Bible about the act of sexual intercourse itself. As we have already observed, the language used to describe the sex act is extravagant and celebratory. The mysterious oneness produced when two people become physically one is described, not with the slushy sentimentality of the pop song, not with the all-too-inadequate metaphor of the poem or the ballad, but with the most superlative imagery man could conceive of. Paul likens this act of love to the relationship Jesus has with his Bride, the Church (Ephesians 5:31–32) which, in turn, is likened to the relationship which has always existed between God the Father and God the Son (John 15:9). Not only that, Paul implies that this is a two-way picture. Sexual union is like this God-Bride relationship and the God-Bride relationship may best be thought of with this physical fusion in mind. You cannot have a higher view, or a purer picture of genital bodily fusion, than that.

No. The Bible is never anti-sex. What the Bible does insist on is sexual intercourse in the relationship for which it was designed: marriage. The Bible knows of only one context for genital fusion and that is the marriage relationship. Even couples who were betrothed to each other – and betrothal was a relationship far more binding than engagement is in the West today – were not permitted to complete their bodily union until after the marriage ceremony had taken place. That is one reason why Joseph was so embarrassed when he discovered Mary's pregnancy. That is one reason why he planned to divorce her secretly.

We shall go on to explore the vexed question 'Why?: Why restrict something so enriching to one relationship in life?' First, let me underline the Bible's prohibition on extra-marital genital activity.

Adultery, promiscuity, lust, homosexuality
The Bible uses four words to describe extra-marital genital intercourse: adultery, promiscuity, lust and homosexuality. We shall look at homosexuality in a later chapter. Here, we look at the other three in turn.

By adultery the Bible means sexual intercourse between a

married person and someone to whom that person is not married. Of adultery, the Bible has this to say:

Exodus 20:14 – 'You shall not commit adultery'

Deuteronomy 5:18 – 'You shall not commit adultery'

Matthew 19:18 – 'You shall not commit adultery'

Romans 13:9 – 'You shall not commit adultery'

The message could not be clearer if it was flashed on our bedroom wall in fluorescent lighting. Do not indulge in sexual intercourse with a person who is married to someone else.

The biblical writers are equally agreed about casual sex. Modern translators use the term sexual immorality to translate the word found in the older texts, 'fornication'. Fornication means genital intercourse with someone to whom you are not married. The Bible insists that this kind of behaviour is not permissible for one who calls himself a Christian:

1 Corinthians 6:13 – 'The body is not meant for sexual immorality, but for the Lord'

1 Corinthians 6:18 – 'Flee from sexual immorality'

Colossians 3:5 – 'Put to death. . .sexual immorality, impurity, lust, evil desires. . .'

1 Thessalonians 4:3 – 'Avoid sexual immorality'

Look up the word 'fornication' in a concordance and complete the list for yourself. I have selected just a few references, enough to show that the New Testament writers are as persuaded as the writer of Genesis seems to be that it is better to lose your coat, your job and your liberty than to lose your virginity (see Genesis 39:12).

Jesus, as always, goes further and deeper. He challenged his followers not simply to set a watch over their behaviour with the opposite sex but to be far more radical. He threw out a startling challenge: Watch your thought-life; the nerve-centre for trouble-shooting operations lies there. As Jesus himself expressed it, ' "You have heard that it was said, 'Do not commit adultery.' But I tell you that everyone who looks at a woman lustfully has already committed adultery with her in his heart" ' (Matthew 5:28). Peter reiterates this command of Jesus: 'Do not give in to bodily passions, which are always at war against the soul' (1 Peter 2:11 GNB). Timothy, likewise, warns us to 'Avoid the passions of youth' (2 Timothy 2:22). As I underlined in chapter two, these verses are not saying, 'Repress your glandular urges'. They are saying, 'Channel them so that they are put to appropriate use, not to destructive use.' To lust means to dwell on the desire for someone's body, to feed on that desire, to give in to inappropriate desires by stealing what is not yours to take. Lust always contains an element of greed and grabbing for the purposes of self-gratification. And Jesus says of this activity, 'Don't!'

This command of Jesus is not easy to obey. If we are to succeed in obeying him, therefore, we must choose carefully the kind of places we visit, the kind of activities we indulge in and the kind of people we allow to influence us.

Why play the waiting game?

If everything we have said so far is true: that God is not the divine spoil-sport; that sex of itself is good; that God's context for sex is marriage, there must be a missing link. We must now try to find it by asking an important question: Why is the context for sexual intercourse marriage and marriage only?

From a vast variety of reasons, I propose to consider two.

First, we must ask ourselves what genital intercourse really is. For too long the myth has been spread abroad that sexual intercourse means simply release of tension, ejaculation of sperm, the contentment of the orgasmic experience. Sexual intercourse does include all this but so much more. Far from being an animalized act, it is also a language capable of conveying profound messages, albeit non-verbally. Within the context of marriage, it conveys the soothing message, 'You are uniquely special to me.' Within the context of marriage, it conveys the healing message, 'I find my place of belonging, my reason for being, in you.' Within the context of marriage, it is the language of permanent, unending, faithful love which alone can eliminate the fear of rejection and the pain of abandonment.

Second, we must consider what the ideal of marriage is. Marriage, as God planned it, means commitment, permanence, fidelity. It means tenderness, understanding, the cluster of intimacies we looked at in chapter one.

Put these two superlatives together: a superlative, non-verbal language of love (non-verbal because it transcends the world of words), and a superlative uniting relationship, and you begin to understand the metaphor Paul uses when he reminds us that the genital union was intended, by the divine architect, to reflect the depth of the oneness and the degree of the commitment and the mystery of the relationship which have always existed between God the Father and God the Son. Genital fusion in any context other than marriage can never ever begin to reflect this wonder, this mystery, this other-worldliness. In any other context it is therefore second-best, and God does not want his children either to taste the bitter dregs of the second-best or to be content with this substitute for the real thing.

No. God intended that, within the relationship he designed to alleviate man's aloneness, this act should symbolize the cementing of that union. When two people fuse their bodies, they transcend their individuality by becoming literally one flesh.

The swing of the pendulum

We live in an interesting phase of our sexual history. If the 1960s go down in history as the peak of the sexual revolution, the 1980s should be noted for the beginning of the counter-revolution. It is not just in the counselling room that people are admitting that sexual experimentation results, not in fullness but in emptiness. Playboys, journalists and personalities as influential as the feminist, Germaine Greer, are drawing their own conclusions in the aftermath of the sexual orgies of the past twenty years.

George Leonard, a journalist writing in a well-known women's magazine, made this admission not very long ago:

> Like millions of others, I welcomed the sexual revolution of the 'sixties with open arms. I even did my own part, through articles, to further it. How healthy, how long overdue this revolution seemed! After years – centuries – of repression, we were now to be free to discuss sexual matters in mixed company, to live together openly without being married, to obtain sexual information easily, to see erotic films and read erotic books, to try out previously forbidden acts and share erotic fantasies with our mates. The revolution enjoyed one swift victory after another. . . .We were on our way to an erotic utopia where informed, mutually consenting individuals could fully realise themselves sexually without public opprobrium or private guilt.[3]

George Leonard goes on to describe his about-turn, the gradual realization that to remove recreational genital intercourse, sex as sport, from all other social and ethical considerations, to divorce it from the context of 'empathy, compassion, morality, responsibility and sometimes even common politeness', resulted in the crudity which may be summed up in three sentences: 'Boy meets girl. Boy gets girl. They part.' And George Leonard comes to this rather moving conclusion:

> Advancers of multiple sex have a saying: 'Why should I be satisfied with a sandwich when there's a feast out there?' They ask this because they have never experienced High Monogamy. Those of us who have tried both tend to see it differently. Casual recreational sex is hardly a feast – not even a good, hearty sandwich. It is a diet of fast food served in plastic containers. Life's feast is available only to those who are willing and able to engage life on a deeply personal level, giving all, holding back nothing. . . .For those who can make the leap of commitment, the rewards are great: a rare tenderness, an exaltation, a highly

charged erotic ambience, surprise on a daily basis, transformation. . . .[4]

Reflections like the above are not rare these days. They are becoming commonplace. They underline, from the poverty of man's experience, the wisdom of the God who would protect us from the effects of this trivialization of the sacred sex act.

To protect us from harm

'To protect? From what?' God, I believe, wants to protect us from the harm which comes so frequently to those who abuse genital love-play, who snatch it out of context for self-gratification. We must now observe some of the harmful effects which have scarred the lives of young men and women.

Genital intercourse, as I have said, is the non-verbal language God created for married couples to communicate that consoling message, 'You are unique – special.' This specialness is the language of permanence. It is intended to be. Remove the act from context and you have that most deeply disturbing of all emotions: the pain of abandonment.

If you have ever seen a rag doll lying on the garden lawn, dirty, soggy from rain or dew, soiled, and if you have ever wondered how it might feel to be such a discarded toy, you are very near an accurate identification with the feeling of abandonment which sweeps over people who have allowed, or been forced to allow, their bodies to be used by another under the pseudonym of 'love' and who have then been relegated to the proverbial scrap-heap.

I encounter the anguish such people experience time and again in my counselling work. I think of the girl who told me she had had intercourse with her boyfriend because she thought he felt about her the same depth of love she felt for him. The day after they had slept together he admitted: 'There's nothing in it as far as I'm concerned. I just know where to touch a girl to make her sexually excited.' Or I think of the girl whose 'friend' forced sexual intimacies on her. 'I tried to scream but I was so frightened, the scream froze on my lips. The next day he apologized saying he thought all girls wanted it. It hadn't occurred to him I might not be one of them.'

To have been used, abused, then tossed aside is not only terrifying: it is devastating. It drives people to drink, to drugs, to suicide in an attempt to block out the pain which refuses to go away. And God, far from being a spoil-sport, wants to protect us from this kind of pain.

And boys are not exempt from the pain: 'After Ruth told me she didn't love me any more, I was stunned. I remember walking and walking round the park, trying to make sense of it all. The hurt inside seemed more than I could take.'

VD

The already high incidence of VD in Britain increases yearly. Contrary to common belief, VD cannot be contracted from toilet seats, soiled towels or dirty sheets; it can only be contracted through sexual involvement with someone who is already carrying the disease.

Venereal disease is serious. Gonorrhoea, the disease which is ever on the increase, produces a severe inflammation of the sex organs and unless it is treated early and effectively, can cause serious damage to the genital tracts of both men and women.

Gonorrhoea of the throat is also on the increase. This, too, is caused by sexual activity: oral sex. In oral sex the girl admits her boyfriend's penis into her mouth and caresses it with her lips and tongue and the male stimulates his girlfriend's clitoris with his mouth and tongue.

Oral sex has been described as 'the sex fad of the seventies'.[5] Popularized by glossy magazines, sex books, blue movies and so-called art, the craze continues into the eighties. As Dr Miriam Stoppard discovered in 1982 when writing her book *Talking Sex*, 'quite a few of you have experienced some kind of oral sex by the time you're sixteen.'[6] This is frightening, because it is now an established fact that oral sex can be dangerous to health if indulged in with a partner who has contracted VD. If the mucous membrane in the mouth comes into contact with a diseased sex organ, then the disease gonorrhoea of the throat may develop. Some medical researchers also believe that a person with a cold sore on the lip who indulges in oral-genital sex may be responsible for transmitting venereal disease.[7]

In addition to the dangers of contracting VD, we must consider the danger of cancer of the cervix. Medical research over the past few years has shown that cancer of the neck of the womb (the cervix) is far more common amongst girls who have indulged in genital intercourse with several partners than in those who have abstained. It is believed that the neck of the womb during the teenage years is highly sensitive, and exposure to semen, particularly if the semen is from a variety of partners, increases the likelihood of a cancerous condition developing. It follows that teenage girls who sleep around automatically place themselves at risk: the risk of developing cancer.

God wants to protect us from this wastage of life, from these debilitating diseases. The answer is not to use the sheath but to keep genital intercourse within the context God has ordained: the committed relationship of marriage.

Pregnancy

And, to add to the perils above, there is always the possibility that the girl will conceive a child. No contraceptive device is foolproof.

I happened to be travelling from Cambridge to Nottingham on Saturday 12 May 1984 and, to while away the time in the 'Little Chef', I picked up a copy of the *Daily Mail*. Two headlines in particular caught my eye:

'Girl, 15, who killed baby is set free'.

'For my baby, the mother you will never see'.

I quote from the first account: 'A tragic schoolgirl who stabbed her secret baby to death was freed by a judge yesterday.

'Mr Justice Webster heard how the 15-year-old girl kept her unwanted pregnancy a secret from her parents and classmates for nine months.

'Finally, while recovering from the birth just before Christmas, she repeatedly stabbed her new-born daughter.

'The girl's mother discovered her daughter's horrifying

secret four days later and found the body in a plastic bag. She called the police.

'Mr. Stephen Wayne, defending, said at Oxford Crown Court: "She has labelled herself a murderess and needs a considerable amount of help. . . ."'

'The girl left the court in the arms of her parents.'

The second account described the reaction of a nineteen-year-old mother to an Appeal Court injunction that her four-year-old daughter should be adopted by foster parents. The mother had made a tape-recording which will be kept by solicitors until her daughter is eighteen years old. The newspaper records: 'Fighting back the tears, the nineteen-year-old said . . . ."I just had to let my little girl know how much I love her. It's terrible I may never see her again and that she won't hear the tape until she's about the age I am now." '

These two heart-breaking situations 'happened' to be recorded in the same newspaper. That same week I had been asked for help by several Christian girls: one who had suffered the indignity of a back-street abortion, another whose baby (conceived out of wedlock) had miscarried. Both girls had kept their secret completely private.

And God wants to protect us from the need to conceal these ghastly secrets. God wants to protect us from the kind of anguish the two teenage mothers I have mentioned must have gone through and will continue to go through for years to come.

God's protection of others

But it is not just the individual God is concerned with. We have seen already in this book the truth of John Donne's claim, 'No man is an island'. Whatever we do, or fail to do, has repercussions for others.

Think back to those tragedies highlighted in the newspaper. Think of a new-born baby being butchered to death; of a four-year-old girl being deprived of her mother. Think of the thousands of unwanted children who are born into this world and who bleat for most of their lives, 'I didn't *ask* to be born'. God would protect innocent children from the pain of a loveless future; the foetus from a premature death.

Or think of the parents of that teenage murderess. How long will it take them to recover? Will they ever recover? Think of the parents of any young person who brings an unwanted child into the world. God wants to protect parents of teenagers and young adults from the pain and shame, the strain and blame this trauma almost always brings in its wake.

No. God is not a spoil-sport God. Love is what God is: protective, discerning, all-wise love. That is why genital intercourse, according to the Bible's teaching, knows of only one context: marriage.

Love your neighbour as yourself

It is customary today to teach teenagers to believe that as long as you love your partner, any kind of genital sport is acceptable. Miriam Stoppard seems to condone the views expressed by teenagers in reply to her questionnaire:

'When is heavy petting OK?

'Girls: usually only when you love the boy. Not on the first date.

'Boys: Quite a lot of boys hope it will be on the first or second date.

'How old should you be?

'Girls: No particular age, only when you love the boy.
'Boys: By fifteen.'[8]

But the question needs to be asked, what *does* this over-worked word 'love' mean? Does it mean the warm feelings which permeate every particle of your being when you have fallen in love? Surely not! Those feelings disappear like smoke in a breeze. This must never be the working definition of love used by Christian couples. Rather, Jesus' definition should be the framework within which we operate: 'Love your neighbour as yourself.'

A person who loves himself never inflicts unnecessary harm on his body, never puts himself in the way of an activity which will sear the conscience, maybe for ever. Shall we, then, condone practices which might bring untold harm to our partner and still call it *love*? Moreover, shall we, in the name of love, risk bringing little lives into the world only to abandon them to children's homes, foster parents or adoptive parents? (I am not belittling the marvellous ministry of many surrogate parents. I am underlining the sheer irresponsibility of behaviour which precipitates the need for such people.)

Moreover, as Christians we have a responsibility to our parents: to love them, respect them, honour them. Can we, as Christians, then, add our voice to those who claim: 'I'm a BIG girl now. I'm going to stop worrying about what my mother says and enjoy this moment'? I think not.

As Christians we have a decision to make. Jim Wallis puts it well, 'Each generation of believers must decide whether their Christianity will have anything to do with Jesus.'[9] A Christian is one who has enlisted for the kingdom of God. A Christian is one who knows Jesus as Lord. And a Christian is one who should therefore obey the King. The tragedy is that, today, among the countless Bible-believing, Jesus-accepting Christians, only a minority are Bible-observing, Jesus-obeying Christians. That is why I say we have a decision to make. In the words of Joshua 24:15, 'If serving the Lord seems undesirable to you, then choose for yourselves this day whom you will serve, whether the gods your forefathers served. . .or the gods . . .in whose land you are living'. A free paraphrase of that verse might read like this: 'Choose for yourselves this day whom you will serve: the goddess of the world in which you live: sex, or King Jesus.' But we cannot serve both, as we shall continue to observe in the next chapter.

Notes for chapter five

1. Margery Williams, *The Velveteen Rabbit* (Heinemann, 1977), pp.14–15.
2. Miriam Stoppard, *Talking Sex* (Piccolo Books, 1982), pp.60–61.
3. George Leonard, 'Sex without Love : Is it enough?' (*Woman's Journal*, March 1983), p.54.

4. 'Sex without Love', p.56.
5. Tim La Haye, *The Act of Marriage* (Zondervan, 1976), p.296.
6. *Talking Sex*, p.75.
7. *The Act of Marriage*, p.279.
8. *Talking Sex*, p.58.
9. Jim Wallis, *The Call to Conversion* (Lion Publishing, 1981), p.xiv.

6
Drawing the Petting Line

'Surely there's room in the Christian faith to make your own decisions about things?' This was one of the many questions contained in the letter I quoted more fully in chapter five. The answer to that question is both 'Yes' and 'No'. Within the framework God has built for our protection there is a great deal of scope for personal decision-making. But where my wants conflict with God's clear commands, like 'You shall not commit adultery', 'Flee sexual immorality', 'Avoid lust', we have no bargaining power. As citizens of God's kingdom, expecting to enjoy all the privileges such citizenship affords, our duty is to obey. And I sometimes wonder what earthly king would accommodate the same degree of rebellion we mete out to God. In Alice-in-Wonderland terms, 'Off with his head' would have been the order of the day!

We saw in the last chapter that God's framework, sexually speaking, rules out pre-marital intercourse for the Christian. This still leaves some pressing problems for the couple in love: Then where do we draw the petting line? How do we control the sex urge? Why do we fail so frequently? What do we do about such frequent failures?

The petting line
A girl once asked me this question: 'If we can't go all the way, how far can we go? What is an appropriate expression of affection in these one-to-one relationships?'

Here is a very important question. You may be reading this chapter because you are searching for an answer to it for yourself or for your friends. It is a question most Christian teachers shelve. I want to tackle it realistically, biblically and frankly. My frankness arises, not from a desire to titillate but to educate. It concerns me that, in the sex-saturated society in which we live, too many Christians are uninformed and compromise their behaviour standards through naiveté.

What I plan to do is to draw a scale and place petting practices in some sort of order on it. We shall then examine some of these activities in detail and I shall try to help you to decide whether these should or should not find a place in your relationships. I am placing the responsibility on *you* (*your* choice, *your* decision) quite deliberately because, although I have said we need to tackle the question biblically, we need to be aware that the petting problem is a twentieth-century problem. The Bible does not address itself to it. One reason for this, as we observed in the preface, is that in the Holy Land, in the days when the Bible was written, marriages were arranged by the parents. A child of three years old might therefore be betrothed to a seemingly suitable partner whom she might not meet until her wedding night. The wedding would probably be solemnized when she was about twelve years old: before the age of puberty. And who wants to start petting before puberty? The Bible writers had no need, then, to address themselves to our sex problems.

In the absence of the specific teaching many of us long for, we must hang as the back-cloth to human reasoning the working definition of love we observed at the end of chapter five: Jesus' command to love your neighbour as yourself. We must also ask ourselves a pertinent question:

'Is my *chief* concern to live biblically or am I wanting to squeeze as much sexual licence as I possibly can out of a holy God?' Pause to put that question to yourself before you read on.

The sliding scale

I realize you cannot really draw an accurate slide-rule or ladder of physical contact; that a warm hug on one occasion may be less erotic than the touch of a hand on another. But I believe a visual aid might help our discussion even though it is an inadequate or, in some senses, an inaccurate one.

It might look something like this:

Genital intercourse
Oral sex
Mutual masturbation
Heavy petting
Petting
Prolonged kissing
Kissing
Cuddling
Embracing
Holding hands

Scale of touch 1

We have already observed that the Bible's teaching on the context of sexual intercourse implies that Bible-observing Christians will draw the line *below* genital intercourse. That is, they will exclude it from their pre-marital experience. The scale will therefore look like this:

Genital intercourse

Oral sex
Mutual masturbation
Heavy petting
Petting
Prolonged kissing
Kissing
Cuddling
Embracing
Holding hands

Scale of touch 2

Thus far the position is clear, though perhaps not welcome to those who wish the Bible was not so definite. But what about the rest of the scale?

Oral sex

Most Bible-believing Christians accept that intercourse is God's wedding present for *married* couples, to be unpacked on the wedding night and enjoyed within the commitment of marriage. But what of oral sex?

Oral sex, as we have seen, takes place when a girl receives her boyfriend's penis into her mouth or when a man caresses his girlfriend's clitoris with his mouth and tongue. Prolonged oral stimulation of this nature can bring both partners to a climax. Technically, this is not full intercourse. Virginity is not lost. Is it then permissible or not?

When you are making up your mind on any course of action in the area of sexual relationships it is important to ask four pressing questions and to place them alongside the biblical principle I have already emphasized: love your neighbour as yourself. The first question to ask is, 'Is this practice dangerous in any way?' The second, 'Does it reflect the nature of Christian love?' Third, 'How does this behaviour, if I indulge in it, affect my spiritual life?' Fourth, 'Is this practice natural, that is, did God design us to make love in this way?' We must address ourselves to each of these questions in turn.

One of the dangers of oral sex is that VD of the throat may be contracted through this activity. Gonorrhoea of the throat is a serious and horrid disease and it is on the increase in our society today. If there is even a vague possibility that this sexual activity will result in disease, is it truly *loving* to subject your partner to this kind of activity?

And what about the nature of Christian love? When Jesus told us to love one another in the same way as he loves us, he expected us to take responsibility for those we say we love. We will therefore avoid inflicting hurt on them, refuse to put them at risk and avoid exposing them to danger. We will refuse to act selfishly or to gratify ourselves. But when it comes to oral sex, I believe many men, in particular, do behave selfishly. They demand a series of sex thrills from their partner which leaves the girl feeling frustrated, bewildered and even nauseated. This, surely, is not love but the antithesis of the kind of love Jesus is describing.

And the effect on your spiritual life must not be ignored. Several couples known to me believed this practice was harmless until they tried it. It quickly drove a wedge between themselves and God. To quote just one couple: 'We believed that oral sex was perfectly all right until we tried it. Then we were plagued with so much guilt that it fouled our relationship with God.'

Any practice which imperils your peace with God should be terminated. It will never be easy to backtrack if you have aroused one another in this way. It will therefore be necessary to talk frankly to your partner and to help one another to re-draw the boundaries of touch.

Christian opinion is divided when it comes to our fourth question, 'Is oral sex natural?' Not everyone will agree with John White's conclusion: 'Orogenital "climaxes" and penile-rectile "climaxes" are *sub*-normal sexual practices. Like masturbation they thwart the erotic culmination for which our bodies were designed, and therefore downgrade sexuality.'[1] In fact, another Christian doctor gives contradicting advice to *married* couples: 'If both of you enjoy it (oral sex) and find it pleasant, then it may properly fit into your lovemaking practices.'[2]

When *married couples* ask my advice about oral sex I echo this second opinion. But I would not give this advice to couples in casual relationships. Surely, such intimacies, if they feature at all, should be reserved for a deeply committed relationship? Surely, if there is even the slightest possibility of VD spreading to your partner through this practice, it should be avoided at all costs?

Mutual masturbation to orgasm

It often happens that two people who love each other agree to abstain from full genital intercourse but, while withholding the final act, the penetration of the vagina by the penis, they stimulate one another's sex organs with the hands until each partner is brought to a full orgasmic experience. Again, technically, intercourse has not taken place and the question is often asked: 'Is this practice permissible or deceitful?'

Again we must consider the dangers of this practice and

measure them against the 'Love your neighbour as yourself' principle. As I explained in my book *Growing into Love*[3], one danger is that a child can be conceived in this way even though the penis never fully penetrates the vagina. Two people indulging in this kind of love-play obviously lie very close and as they arouse one another they move even closer together, so close that sperm may be spilt into the entrance of the vagina. This sperm, though spilt accidentally, is sufficient to fertilize the female egg and thus to conceive a child.

The second danger attached to this practice proves the truth of the saying that sexual kicks have sexual kick-backs. Many couples suffer the deprivation of sexual frigidity after they marry because of this kind of activity in earlier years. The female grows accustomed to manual manipulation and dislikes the change to penile stimulation, and her reluctance to change annoys her husband; the male may be troubled by what is known as premature ejaculation because he has not learned the art of true lovemaking: making his partner happy sexually by waiting before releasing sperm and enjoying a climax for himself. Where this problem persists, the wife feels frustrated, even cheated.

Of course, I am not saying that all couples who practise mutual masturbation to orgasm will bring a child into the world, nor that all such couples will meet sexual adjustment problems after they are married. What I am saying is that very many people do suffer in this way and the question therefore needs to be posed: Is this responsible loving? Is it loving at all? Is it responsible? Isn't it a pharisaical keeping of the letter of the law while denying the spirit of it? I have discussed this further in *Growing into Love*, p.87.

As Christians we owe it to one another not to scar others emotionally. This practice frequently does. As Christians we are exhorted to honour our parents. The degree of pain inflicted on parents by pregnancies of this nature is heartbreaking. As Christians we owe it to society not to bring unwanted children into the world. Can this behaviour, therefore, be indulged in by Christians and leave them guilt-free? And, again, we must enquire what effect this genital excitation has on each individual's walk with God.

Each individual must decide for himself. But in my opinion, one-to-one relationships of the kind we are studying, which are formed without any probability of marriage, years away from the possibility of marriage, should push the boundary even further back so that the sliding scale begins to look like this:

Genital intercourse

Oral sex

Mutual masturbation

?————————?

Heavy petting

Petting

Prolonged kissing

Kissing

Cuddling

Embracing

Holding hands

Scale of touch 3

Heavy petting

By heavy petting I mean the practice of slipping your hands inside a girl's dress to fondle her breasts; or undoing the zip of your boyfriend's trousers to fondle his genitals; or stroking your girlfriend's thighs or genitalia. Heavy petting includes lying together in a state of undress from the waist upwards, or fully naked; lying side by side or on top of one another.

There is nothing wrong with these activities *of themselves*. They are the delights designed by God for marriage where they are intended to result in intercourse, created to awaken the degree of sexual excitation which will eventually bring each partner to orgasm.

As Christian people we must be responsible people. As Christian people we must learn to make wise choices. As Christian people we must look ahead, not just at passing pleasures, but at their consequences. Anyone who has crossed the boundary between petting, by which I mean fondling one another outside the clothes, and the heavy petting I have just described, will tell you, if they are honest, that the difference is phenomenal: it is not unlike the difference between grinding along in second gear and slipping into overdrive.

We need to acknowledge the cold, clinical fact of the matter that there is something about the naked flesh which brings to the surface the full force of sexual desire, the glandular urge we talked about in chapter two. As one girl described it to her boyfriend when his hands started wandering down her body: 'There's a tigress living inside me, and if you touch me there it will leap out at us.' She was right.

That tiger has to be tamed; not chained, nor mounted and ridden, but trained. Tiger-training becomes much more difficult with every new and exciting form of touch. That is why you may have to bring the boundaries back another notch:

Genital intercourse

Oral sex
Mutual masturbation
Heavy petting

?————————?

Petting
Prolonged kissing
Kissing
Cuddling
Embracing
Holding hands

Scale of touch 4

- Genital intercourse is for marriage only.
- Consider carefully the consequences of breaking into the question mark areas.
- Think carefully about the effect of every expression of affection. Don't *assume* that any form of touch is necessarily innocent for you.

Petting

By petting I mean fondling one another's breasts and genitals outside the clothes. I also mean any form of lying together. Included in petting comes prolonged kissing: any kiss which is more than a leisurely peck and particularly any kiss which involves that highly sensitive organ, the tongue.

What we have to recognize is that any form of petting is dynamite. As one young friend of mine admitted after kissing his girlfriend for the first time: 'It was fantastic. But it was frightening too. It brought to the surface such powerful feelings in me that I didn't even know were there. I know I'm going to have to cool it or I will lose control.'

I admire a young person who admits to that degree of pressure and adjusts the sexual sliding scale accordingly. As I said at the beginning of this chapter, the Bible does not set out a neat set of rules. 'Do not indulge in petting.' 'Do not kiss for more than thirty seconds.' 'Abstain from cuddling, caressing and holding hands.' The Bible does not even mention these fascinating phenomena for reasons I explained earlier.

In the absence of absolute guidelines, every Christian young person must take stock of the bare, biological facts: Holding hands quickly leads to embracing. Embracing leads to cuddling, caressing and kissing almost as quickly. This first, fairly innocent, phase passes automatically, yet imperceptibly, into the next: petting. Once the body is thus revved up, it wants to dictate the pace, to press on to pursue the delights of heavy petting. But by the time a couple indulges in heavy petting, chemical changes have taken place which make it exceedingly difficult for most people to stop short of intercourse.

For example, when a man fondles his girlfriend's breasts, her nipples swell and become highly sensitive to touch. At the same time a secretion of fluid lubricates her vagina so that her body is prepared for the act of intercourse. God did not create the female body with a convenient off-switch which could be applied at the height of sexual excitation.

Similarly, when a girl fondles her boyfriend's genitals, the penis becomes stiff and highly sensitive to touch. When aroused by such an erection, the male, no matter how sincerely he *desires* to go God's way, finds it extremely hard to say no to the full act of intercourse. Again, God seems not to have supplied the male body with a switch which can be flicked to 'off' when the pressure is on.

I have spelt out these cold, clinical facts, not to shock, but to educate. If we are to be adult and to make wise and loving choices we must know the facts, be aware of the dangers, heed the warnings and act accordingly.

Young people sometimes press me for an answer to the question, 'How far *can* we go?' I realize that if you are one of those people, if you are reading this chapter because you want me to decide for you where you should draw the petting line, you may well be feeling disappointed and frustrated by now. I hope, though, that you will accept that I cannot be your conscience.

On biblical authority I have the right to say to you that genital intercourse outside of marriage is wrong. I have no *biblical* authority for dictating to you where you draw the petting line. What I do have is the responsibility, as an older Christian, not to leave you to muddle your way through your relationships with the opposite sex; the compassion to encourage you to think carefully about your use of touch.

While I was planning this chapter I was invited to speak to a certain Christian Union group. On my way to the meeting, I drove along a stretch of road which had been newly surfaced. Road signs warned drivers to restrict their speed to 20 mph. But several drivers speeded past me at 60 mph. I was not surprised, therefore, to find the roadside littered with fragments of shattered windscreens. In this chapter I have tried to point out the dangers. Whether or not you slow down is entirely up to you; but if you decide to accelerate, be aware of the possible consequences for you and your partner and your relationship with God.

Cooling the sex urge

But *how* do you slow down? How *do* you cool it? When the flame of passion begins to burn, how do you quench it? Where is the fire extinguisher? Or as one girl put it, 'What I'd like to know is *how* – how do you channel your sexuality into forging warm friendships? If you don't repress or suppress your genital desires, then surely they'll take over – especially at certain stages of the menstrual cycle when you only have to touch your skin and your body tingles all over?'

In responding to this question I want us to look at certain provocative situations to avoid, certain substitutes which might replace excessive cuddling and certain disciplines which must be introduced if we are to master our sexual desires instead of being consumed by them.

As we observed in chapter two, any appetite grows when it is fed. The more you eat, the more you want to eat until you overeat unless you control your appetite. The same is true of the sex appetite. Yet Christians may develop, as others do, an inflated interest in sex. They may feast on plays, novels, girlie magazines, blue movies, pictures of pin-ups, and personal erotic fantasies. We are surrounded by people who are prepared to go on feeding our insatiable sex hunger. There is money in it. Paul's advice is this, 'Don't be beguiled'. Rather, feast on heavenly things while you deliberately deal the death-blow to the lust, the evil, the greed and the idolatry which incurs the wrath of God (see Colossians 3:2 and 5).

Of course, this reorientation will not come naturally nor without a struggle. But just as a diabetic knows that unless he changes his diet he will die, we, too, have to take the sex situation seriously. Unless we act ruthlessly and take ourselves in hand, placating the sex tiger will result in spiritual death for some of us. It is as serious as that.

Situations to avoid

But this reorientation is not simply a reorientation of the mind. It has to be accompanied by a radical change in behaviour. We know, for example, that provocative dress eggs people on, yet Christians (both male and female) sometimes wear jeans specially designed 'to make you sexy'; women wear perfume guaranteed to inflame the passion, see-through blouses which leave little to the imagination, skin-tight T-shirts and no bra, all of which attract attention to the curves so fascinating to the opposite sex. Such provocative dress is not only unwise but unloving. It makes self-control difficult for one's partner and Christians in general.

Similarly, certain behaviour which pretends to be love-in-action is the antithesis of love. As we have seen, petting, and particularly heavy petting, produces the kind of sexual excitation where it is almost impossible to say 'No' to the full act of genital intercourse. Many, many Christian couples have compromised their own sex standards not because they set out to rebel against God, but because in their love-play they reached the point of no return and fell captive to erotic desire and passion. Many have done so in complete ignorance. I feel a deep burden for such couples. That is why I have tried to spell out the facts explicitly, calling a spade a spade in this way. Keep these facts before you. Know which are the highly sensitive, erogenous zones on your body: the breasts, the nipples, the thighs, the genitals, even the ear lobes! If your partner's hands stray on to these areas, push them away, tenderly but firmly. As Walter Trobisch so sensibly said, 'A slap on the fingers can be a greater proof of love than a French kiss.'[4] And if your partner pushes that hand away, show them that you respect them by keeping the hand away. To inflict unwanted genital intimacy on anyone, or to charm another person to go further than they want to go, is not love, it is selfishness. It means you care more about yourself than your partner. Love never trespasses, never tries to take advantage of another, never tries to overpower another, or to borrow Len Barnett's phrase, never tries to 'storm the gate'. No. Real love is patient, kind, protective of the loved one's safety and well-being.

And real love recognizes the fact of the situation, that nakedness, near-nakedness and any form of undressing is in itself a powerful stimulus. It quickly brings couples to that point of no return I referred to earlier.

I am not saying be scared silly by these facts. Nor am I saying sweep them under the carpet as though they do not exist. I am not even saying sit on them. What I am saying is, recognize their powerful presence. Recognize that they are a God-given part of you. Resolve, not to be mastered by them, but to be good stewards of them.

Stewarding your sexuality

You can do this in three ways: by controlling your desires, disciplining them and replacing a glut of genital play with other activities. Let me explain what I mean.

The most successful disciplinarian among the school-teachers who taught me at school was the smallest, quietest, most mouselike teacher in the school. She would often arrive to find our form in uproar. Faced with the riot, she never seemed to panic. She certainly never shouted. She did use a foolproof method of class discipline. She would stand at her desk, peer at the rebellious class, sum up the situation and then whisper in her soft, prim voice, 'I want you all to stand by your desks and be quite silent.' We always fell for it. Because she spoke in a whisper, an insistent 'Shh! Shh!' would go round the classroom. To hear her was to obey her. And so we would stand, sheepish and still, beside our desks. Meanwhile she, like Little Bo-Peep, would gaze at us with a hurt expression which seemed to say, 'How could you do this to me?' We would feel guilty. The hubbub would subside. Then she would smile her beautiful smile and say, 'Now sit down and take out your books.' As I say, we fell for it every time.

Our glandular urges, the biological tension which pulsates through our body, the sexual desire which surges through our minds and emotions threatening to devour our entire person, like a class of rowdy, rebellious teenagers, can be controlled and disciplined. We must not suppress them. We must not repress them, as I said earlier. We must acknowledge their presence and determine that, like my timid teacher, we *will* gain the upper hand.

We must do this because Jesus requires it of us and to love him is to obey him (John 14:15). We must do this because love can be hurt, even killed, by mis-directed sex. We must do this for our own well-being. The million dollar question is, 'How?'.

One way is to follow Paul's advice to the Philippians. 'Whatever is true, whatever is noble, whatever is right, whatever is pure, whatever is lovely, whatever is admirable – if anything is excellent or praiseworthy – think about such things' (Philippians 4:8). In other words, retune your minds. Tune out the distorted. Tune into the truth.

Genital love-play, as we have seen, *is* true and noble and pure and lovely and admirable and excellent and praise-worthy and right in its God-given context, marriage. Because it is tarnished and trivialized and cheapened when snatched out of this context, we have to learn in our one-to-one pre-marital relationships, the art of focusing, not primarily on the physical expression of affection, but on the many other ingredients of the friendship which, it is to be hoped, exist alongside erotic desire. The clamour for genital intercourse is reduced as you determine to explore all the other avenues of your relationship: sport, music, Christian activities, poetry, reading, walking and so on. Concentrate on these and you find that a thousand strands of sharing bind you to one another in a rich relationship. Isolate the physical and over-indulge in it and, like eating too much Devonshire cream on holiday, you will be sick: sick from it and sick of it.

As you refocus, as you determine to gain the mastery, a new sense of excitement creeps into the relationship. You even begin to enjoy that much-neglected art 'discipline'. After all, the discipline of waiting until marriage for the full, physical expression of love is not unlike the discipline of keeping your Christmas presents unopened until Christmas Day. You know your presents sit there, wrapped, on top of the wardrobe. You long for a feel or a peep or a shake. But you know that to let those parcels divulge their secret pre-maturely will spoil the unique magic of Christmas Day. Similarly, as Walter Trobisch so rightly says, those who unwrap God's wedding present of genital intercourse miss the 'beauty of the in-between, the pain of waiting and the joy of suspense, the suffering which made them so happy'.[5] And as Richard Foster reminds us, 'Discipline brings freedom.'[6]

The role of the will
The key to victory is the will. When I pointed this out to the girl who asked the question I quoted at the beginning of this section, 'How do you channel your sexuality into forging warm friendships?', her face brightened, her eyes sparkled

and she replied, 'Yes. It *is* possible, isn't it? I mean, you *can* discipline yourself. It all depends on the will. Perhaps that's where the elusive off-switch hides – in the will.'

Metropolitan Anthony Bloom underlines the vital role played by the will:

> We must be prepared to do God's will and pay the cost. . . .We see that we cannot partake deeply of the life of God unless we change profoundly. It is therefore essential that we should go to God in order that he should transform and change us. . . .But it is not a change of mind alone that we call conversion. We can change our minds and go no farther; what must follow is an act of the will and unless our will comes into motion and is redirected Godwards, there is no conversion; at most there is only an incipient, still dormant and inactive change in us. . . .
>
> Nor does conversion end there: it must lead us farther in the process of making us different. Conversion begins but it never ends. It is an increasing process in which we gradually become more and more what we should be.[7]

With an act of the will, then, we must place the hard clay of our rebellious will into the hands of the Creator and beg him to remould us. To change the metaphor, we must constantly bring our lives into alignment with the will of the Father, or more accurately, ask God to bring our wills into alignment with his. Prayer must become the Alignment Centre. Prayer must be the place where we sweat out the fearsome battle Jesus fought in his temptation in the wilderness. Prayer must become the place where, like Jesus, we make our choice: to live a life centred around number one, gratifying self no matter who gets hurt or deprived, or to deny ourselves the delights of self-gratification so that we fulfil the law of the King.

To align ourselves to the King cannot happen without a struggle. It can be done by struggling, by co-operating with the Holy Spirit, and by the grace of God.

What we must do with these sexual appetites is what we do when we fast from food. You plan a thirty-six-hour fast. At eight o'clock the first morning, your appetite tells you it is time for breakfast. You do not repress the desire by pretending you are not hungry. You look at the clock, admit to your stomach that normally you do eat at this time, but you tell your stomach that today will be different. You are not eating toast for breakfast: simply drinking water. At one o'clock the situation repeats itself. That insistent little voice called appetite knocks on the door of your awareness to remind you it is dinner time. 'So it is,' you reply, gently, with appreciation. 'But today, we're not having the normal fare: just a glass of water.' At six o'clock, appetite, the faithful clock-watcher, visits your awareness again. 'Remember what I said?' you reply. 'We're not eating for another twelve hours. Let's have a glass of water.'

The first time you fast, you wonder whether you and appetite can keep up the contest. The second time you fast, it becomes easier. After that, the routine becomes an adventure. You know you can do it. You know that you are not in bondage to food or appetite. You know that by the grace of God, *you* are in control.

The way to treat the appetite of sex is not dissimilar. Listen to its clamour. Recognize your need. Admit that these urges are not someone else's problems but yours. Then take the emotions in hand. Treat them like rowdy children. Discover the inner freedom which really does come from discipline.

You will not discover it until you try it.

Why do we fail?
'Then why do I fail so consistently?' I can almost hear my readers ask that question. I have a letter on the desk beside me asking just that question. I have a young couple coming to see me this week puzzled by that same question, crushed by persistent failure.

There are so many reasons. There's space here to mention only three: bondage to the world's view, bondage to self, bondage to the robot mentality.

Bondage to the world's view

Many of us, despite what I have written, despite what we believe in our heads, are gripped at gut level by the world's view of sex: love each other and do what you like. In his excellent little booklet, *Love is a Feeling to be Learned,* Walter Trobisch shows how subtly this belief worms its way into our lives:

> During the time of Hitler, a film was shown in Germany which told the story of a doctor whose wife had an incurable disease. In detail the film showed how she was tormented by her sickness until her husband killed her with an overdose of sedatives. When he was put on trial for murder, he defended himself by saying : 'I loved my wife.'
>
> Here, God's commandment: 'Thou shalt not kill' was questioned in the name of love.
>
> The film was shown in 1940 and was used by Hitler as a psychological preparation for the killing of the incurable and insane, for exterminating life which he judged unworthy of living. The end was the assassination of six million Jews in the gas chambers of the concentration camps.

Walter Trobish concludes, and I agree with him,

> If we seek to set up the standard of love ourselves, we fall into the hands of the devil. When Germany questioned the commandment 'Thou shalt not kill' in the name of love, she fell into the hands of the devil. When we question today the commandment 'Thou shalt not commit adultery' in the name of love we fall equally into the hands of the devil.
>
> Since we do not know what love is, love has to be protected by the One who is love himself. There is never a contradiction between love and divine will. There is no action of love which goes against a commandment of God.[8]

When we disobey the King, as Adam found centuries ago, we give Satan a foothold in our lives. He wreaks havoc now as he did then. What we must do, therefore, is to renounce the devil with all his lies and his ways, seek to be cut free from this bondage and determine to live differently.

Bondage to self

The second reason why we may fail is that each of us was born with a bias to pleasing self and with an equally powerful bias against pleasing God. Dietrich Bonhoeffer reminds us that, 'When Christ calls a man, he bids him come and die.' Yes. The self has to die but the self is siow to die. Like the proverbial cat, it seems to have nine lives. We think we have put lust to death one day and the next it proves to us that it is alive and well, as troublesome as ever.

Where the determination to live for self is born of rebellion against God, 'I am *going* to make my own decisions no matter what God says', we need to confess and be cut free from this self-seeking attitude. But it sometimes happens that this search for genital love is born, not so much from rebellion as from deprivation of love in the past or the present. Where sexual immorality springs from deep-seated need, it is healing which is required as well as confession. We shall examine this deprivation of love in more detail in the chapters on homosexuality and on loneliness.

Bondage to the robot mentality

A third reason why Christian couples sometimes push over the boundaries they themselves have built round their genital expression of affection is that they expect God to do what they themselves must learn to do: discipline their thoughts, discipline the wandering fingers, discipline the runaway emotions. One young man I know complains regularly about God in the context of sex: 'I've trusted him with my life. Then why does he allow me to be so wayward?' But this young man puts himself in situations where he knows full well temptation will gain the mastery over his wobbly will. This young man feasts on pictures and thoughts he knows full well will feed his moral weakness. Why, then, blame God? God is not going to padlock our feet, handcuff our hands or clap our wild imagination into prison. No. We are not God's robots, nor are we puppets on God's string. We are adults. Free. Free to make good choices. Free to disobey.

When we fail

And if we disobey, if we fail, what then? Recollections of praying with young people tormented by sexual misdemeanours of the past and present are among my most treasured memories as I reflect on my counselling ministry. The good news which I want to shout from the roof tops, which I have already emphasized in my book *Growing into Love,* is that sexual sin is not the unforgivable sin.

Nevertheless, sexual sin is a grievous sin. As Paul puts it in his pastoral letter to the Corinthians: 'All other sins a man commits are outside his body, but he who sins sexually sins against his own body' (1 Corinthians 6:18). But it is deeper even than that. As we noted earlier, sexual sin sinks in deeply. As one girl put it to me once: 'It's the memories that keep cropping up, the dreams, the guilt. I just *can't* forgive myself even though it all happened years ago.' There are ways out of this predicament. Because they have relevance to later chapters also, I have placed them in a chapter of their own at the end of this book. Turn to it when you need to. Use it. Let it be one of the ways God transforms you into the likeness of his amazing Son.

Notes for chapter six

1. John White, *Eros Defiled* (IVP, 1977), p.25.
2. Ed and Gaye Wheat, *Intended for Pleasure* (Scripture Union, 1977), p.76.
3. Joyce Huggett, *Growing into Love* (IVP, 1982), p.87.
4. Walter Trobisch, *Love is a feeling to be learned* (IVP, 1974), p.25.
5. *Love is a feeling. . .* , p.17.
6. Richard Foster, *Celebration of Discipline* (Hodder and Stoughton, 1980), p.45.
7. Anthony Bloom, *Living Prayer* (Libra, 1973), pp.64–66.
8 Walter Trobisch, *Love is a feeling. . .* , p.21.

7
Mismatched with Unbelievers

Chosen people enjoy certain privileges. But chosen people carry certain responsibilities also.

I discovered this for myself, in a minor way, in 1953 when I was chosen to represent the Girl Guides of Exeter at the Coronation of Queen Elizabeth II. In my case, the requirement was that my shoes should shine as never before, my Girl Guide badge should gleam as never before, and I should look smarter than ever before. Athletes chosen for the 1984 Olympics also discovered the truth that selection and responsibility go together. As one put it, 'We have lived for the Games and made personal sacrifices for them.'

Christians are chosen people. 'You did not choose me, but I chose you' (John 15:16). 'You are a chosen people, a royal priesthood, a holy nation, a people belonging to God' (1 Peter 2:9). 'We know that he has chosen you' (1 Thessalonians 1:4). Christians therefore carry huge responsibilities: 'I chose you to go and bear fruit – fruit that will last' (John 15:16). 'You are a chosen people . . . that you may declare the praises of him who called you out of darkness into his wonderful light' (1 Peter 2:9). We are chosen for obedience: 'Why do you call me, "Lord, Lord," and do not do what I say?' (Luke 6:46). 'Not everyone who says to me, "Lord, Lord," will enter the kingdom of heaven, but only he who does the will of my Father who is in heaven' (Matthew 7:21). Clearly, the Christian is one of whom sacrifice and one-hundred-per-cent loyalty is expected.

All this presents few problems and a whole galaxy of joys until our will clashes with God's will. Then there are tears and tantrums, rebellion and the flat refusal to believe that God not only knows what is best for us but actually has our best interests at heart.

Anna knew this when she came to see me. Even so, as she fought back the tears, she pleaded with me to find a loophole in 2 Corinthians 6:14, which says: 'Do not be mismated with unbelievers' (RSV). 'Isn't there *any* way that Robin and I can get married, Joyce? I love him so much. I really don't want to give him up.' Anna knew what I would say before she came to see me. Even so, when she realized she was fighting a losing battle, she became bitter: 'It's as bad as belonging to a sect or something – not being able to make your own decisions, not being able to please yourself.'

But is it like that? Are God's constraints unreasonable; or do they perhaps make sound sense after all? Does the embargo on mixed marriages extend to the 'going out' phase? In other words, should a Christian 'go out' with a non-Christian? If not, why not? These are the questions we must now grasp firmly by the hand and seek, not simply to answer, but to understand.

Why the embargo on 'mixed marriages'?

First, we must explore what the Bible has to say about the problem of mixed marriages, not racially, but spiritually mixed. To do this, three key passages need to be examined.

First, there is the shrewd question asked by Amos: 'Do two walk together unless they have agreed to do so?' In other words: Do two form a close relationship unless they bring the same set of expectations to their developing friendship? This question, like the others which follow in Amos 3:3ff.: 'Does a lion roar in the thicket when he has no prey? Does he growl in his den when he has caught nothing?' (verse 4), for example, assumes the answer: 'No way'.

Some Bible teachers suggest that this verse applies, not only to friendships and business relationships, but to the marriage relationship also. Whether it does or does not is not clear from the text. What is clear is that two people entertaining marriage will, if they are wise, ensure that their goals in life are compatible. What is also clear is that marriage counsellors today are underlining the imbalance which is created in a marriage relationship when two people marry from different faiths or where a person with a strong faith marries a person for whom faith in God finds no niche in their life. They describe these relationships as high-risk propositions.

Paul's teaching

The passage most Christians turn to when they weigh whether marriage or 'going out' with an unbeliever is permissible or not is 2 Corinthians 6:14–17 where Paul has this to say:

> Do not be yoked together with unbelievers. For what do righteousness and wickedness have in common? Or what fellowship can light have with darkness? What harmony is there between Christ and Belial? What does a believer have in common with an unbeliever? What agreement is there between the temple of God and idols? For we are the temple of the living God. As God has said: "I will live with them and walk among them, and I will be their God, and they will be my people."
>
> "Therefore come out from them and be separate, says the Lord."

Many Bible commentators are convinced that 'The subject-matter here is marriage with unbelievers . . . .The apostle strongly exhorts Christians not to mix with unbelievers in the sense of sharing in their lives. Marriage is, of course, the supreme way of sharing in the life of another.'[1]

The translators contributing to the New English Bible seem so convinced that the relationship in Paul's mind is marriage that they translate verse 14 in this stark way: 'Do not unite yourselves with unbelievers; they are no fit mates for you.' If this translation is accurate, you cannot have it spelt out more clearly than that.

Jesus' teaching

As we observed in chapter two, isolated verses must always

be interpreted in the light of the Bible's wider teaching. For example what did Jesus have to say about mixed marriages? Jesus does not refer to such relationships specifically. What he does do is to take us back to first principles: 'A man will leave his father and mother and be united to his wife, and the two will become one flesh' (Matthew 19:5; *cf.* Genesis 2:24). The oneness of which Jesus speaks here includes genital fusion but its meaning is much broader and deeper than the mere joining of two bodies. Jesus here refers to the emotional oneness, the creative oneness, and the *spiritual oneness* Adam and Eve so clearly enjoyed in the Garden of Eden where together they communed with God in the cool of the day.

Marriage, as Jesus would have it, envisages a foundation of spiritual oneness: a spiritual harmony.

A strait-jacket?

Why? Why does God make this bold, irreversible statement: 'Do not be mismated with unbelievers'? Why does he say unbelievers are not fit mates for Christians? From the many reasons put forward, I propose to dwell on two: one negative, one positive. First, the negative.

The young people in the Youth Group I used to lead pestered me with this question on one occasion. Like Anna, they were up in arms because God's Word did not happen to fit in with their whims. 'Why?' they would ask. 'Why is God so unreasonable, so mean? Why is Christianity so restrictive?'

It so happened that among the members of the Young Wives Group were many who had become Christians after they married, who therefore found themselves in the mixed marriage situation Paul refers to in 1 Corinthians 7:12ff. I decided, therefore, to ask them why they thought God had placed us in this seeming strait-jacket.

Although fifteen years have flashed by since these conversations took place, I still have the notes I made in front of me, and I still recall the look of utter bewilderment which crept over each face as we talked. One woman gave voice to the perplexity they all felt: 'But why should a Christian *want* to marry a non-Christian? There are so many disadvantages, so many heartaches, so many problems.'

They went on to pin-point some of the problems.

'Take Sundays, for example. We're all getting ready for church – the children and me, that is. Bill makes it clear he's not coming. Well! You know what children are. They start asking these embarrassing questions. "Mum! Why isn't dad coming to church? Isn't he a Christian like us?" I really love Bill. I know these things hurt him and I hate seeing him hurt. I try to point out to the children that their father is a *good* man. But it's difficult.'

Another voice added, 'Yes. And there's every meal time. We sit there with the meal on the table. When it's just me and the children we say grace. When their father's there, we all look embarrassed. "Shall we? Shan't we?" I want ours to be a *Christian* home especially for the children's sake, but how can it be while the head of the home is an unbeliever?'

'My problem is that my husband feels threatened by my faith. Oh! I don't mean he stops me praying or reading the Bible, or even going to Young Wives or church once on Sunday. But he doesn't want me getting involved. He actually says that. "Don't you get involved." But I *want* to be involved in the Lord's work.'

'The thing that bothers me is not being able to use my home for God. We've got a lovely home. It could easily be used for the Lord. But Tom won't think of it. It's his castle. He comes in, raises the drawbridge and won't think of sharing it – especially with the church.'

I knew each of these husbands well. They were all pleasant, accommodating, generous people, in many ways the salt of the earth. None of them set out to make life difficult for their wives. The problem was not so much of their making as the nature of the inevitable imbalance a mixed marriage brings. The leaning-tower-of-Pisa syndrome cannot be righted unless the unbelieving partner becomes a Christian or the Christian abandons his or her faith.

This is so obvious, but a stab of pain went right through me when a likeable non-Christian husband spelt this out in my presence recently. He and his Christian wife had been sitting in my lounge bickering for well over an hour. The wife poured out her bitterness at the way her husband failed her constantly. I listened while she hammered him with hurtful home-truths. As we drew the counselling session to a conclusion, this bewildered man made the shrewd comment which cut me to the quick: 'What my wife needs is a *Christian* husband.' He could not have been more accurate. His wife had married him in a rebellious anti-God phase. Since, she had returned to her first love for God but her husband could not match her cherished expectations of what a Christian husband should be because he lacked the essential qualification: a shared faith. Their marriage ended in divorce.

Love for the Lord cements marriages

But there is a positive reason for marrying a Christian who is going the same way with Christ as you are: love for the Lord cements the marriage in a way nothing else can. Indeed, the Lord's love is the frame in which your two loves fit together and which, in fact, holds them together. Look at it this way. If two people walking in a botanic garden are attracted by the same rare flower, they both move towards that flower to examine it. In moving nearer to the flower, they move ever nearer to one another. Similarly, in marriage, if two people are growing ever nearer and ever more like the Lord they love, then imperceptibly they will each be drawing nearer to the other. It cannot be avoided.

This love for the Lord which is central to them both binds them together. It is at the core of their marriage and influences everything they do and are. In such a marriage both work towards the same goal: to serve Christ, to put him first in everything, to conduct their lives within the divine framework. Thus their lives become integrated and this creates harmony in the home.

Going out with a non-Christian

'But I'm not talking about *marriage*. I don't want to marry Mike. I just want to go out with him. Surely there's nothing wrong with that? And perhaps he'll become a Christian through me?'

It's quite true. The non-Christian *might* become a Christian through the witness of the believing partner. A few have done. If the statistics are to be believed, though, this happens only very rarely. What normally happens is that the Christian grows cold and abdicates all his or her responsibilities as a citizen of the kingdom of heaven.

I have personally seen this happen too many times to remain apathetic or unconcerned when someone like Anna, whom I mentioned earlier, comes to see me. I am deeply concerned for Christians who take such dangerous risks.

It still hurts to reflect on the unfolding story of a young friend of mine who gave his life to Christ while studying in this country and who subsequently returned home to resume the friendship he once enjoyed with a non-Christian girl. 'I know what the Bible says about not marrying an unbeliever. I just like her, that's all.'

But he *did* marry her. When I visited them in their own home, I asked him what marriage had done to his faith. A shadow seemed to pass over his face and his eyes grew sad as he admitted: 'I haven't been to church once since my wedding. I never read my Bible these days and scarcely ever pray.'

I looked out of the window and watched his small children playing in the garden. 'And the children?'

'They know nothing whatsoever about the Lord.'

'How do you feel – deep down inside, I mean?'

In reply to that question this young man admitted to the inner sadness, the yawning emptiness which no-one and nothing could fill. 'My faith really mattered to me. Jesus really mattered to me.'

Lop-sided values, beliefs, behaviour patterns
But I have not forgotten that the questioner whom I quoted at the beginning of this section insisted that she was not intending to marry Mike. Doesn't that make a difference? Doesn't the toll-gate swing open if this is not a one-way trip?

I don't think so. Mismating presents huge problems often: problems of lopsided values, beliefs, expectations and behaviour patterns.

Look at it this way. One of the wonderful things about

friends is that they share the same values, or as C.S. Lewis puts it, they see the same truth. The typical expression of such friendship would be something like, ' "What? You too? I thought I was the only one." '[2] Love in this context means that two or more people care about the same realities.

One of the biggest problems with the Christian/non-Christian pairing-off problem is that these two people do not share the same truth: the same value systems, the same guiding principles for life or the same beliefs.

You may retort: 'Does this really matter?' Surely a golf enthusiast can marry a squash player and their relationship need not be damaged; it can be enhanced if one learns to play or watch golf and the other to play or watch squash.

Unfortunately, this is not a neat or accurate parallel. If being a Christian means anything, it means giving God the first place in your life; revolving your life around him. If you go out with an unbeliever, however good and close and enriching the friendship is, an essential element must be missing: the spiritual. As someone summed it up for me the other day: 'being hitched to a non-Christian as I am, I simply cannot be the kind of Christian I want to be.'

It is not simply that a strand is missing; the heart of the relationship is missing. Two Christians can enrich one another's spiritual lives by reading the Bible together, praying together, going to church together, attending meetings together, working for God together. A man looks at spiritual truths differently from a woman. Put together the male and female viewpoints and you have a rich whole. The relationship becomes, not like a flabby lettuce which has no heart, but one which is firm at the centre, healthy, satisfying, growing.

The moral dilemma

But the problem does not centre round absent ingredients. It often introduces a strain on the couple concerned because of what is present: opposite and opposing hopes of the relationship.

Take the genital problems we discussed in chapters two, five and six for example. A Christian, as we have seen, is one who has sworn allegiance to Jesus Christ, one who has enlisted in Jesus' service, who has promised life-long obedience. The unbeliever has made no such choice so neither expects the benefits of becoming a Christian nor expects to pay the price of becoming a Christian.

On the one hand, then, you have a Christian partner who knows that if they are to live biblically they will draw the line this side of pre-marital sex. On the other hand, you have the unbeliever who acknowledges no such restraints; like most unbelievers they might well believe the exact opposite.

I say this, not because I believe all unbelievers are rebellious, therefore promiscuous, but because, if I read the signs of the times correctly, an increasing number of teenagers grow up today believing that pre-marital sex is the norm. I think, for example, of a programme transmitted on television in June 1984 which showed that, since the sex revolution of the 1960s, most teenagers would expect to have sexual intercourse before marriage. Or I think of a report published in May 1984 that claimed that teenage boys in Britain today take as their model James Bond and, in true 007 fashion, try to 'make it' with as many girls as possible; that many girls feel pressurized to prove their femininity by forfeiting their virginity. Girls even feel convinced that to please a man they must permit him to have sex with them; that this behaviour is natural and normal.

This is the current climate in which the Christian co-exists with the non-Christian. We have already observed the peer-group pressure to conform. We have already observed that, for most of us, it is a struggle to abstain from pre-marital genital intercourse with someone who attracts us physically. These pressures are accentuated when someone who takes James Bond as their model mismates with a person who takes Jesus Christ as their model. An *unbeliever* put the situation so clearly when he apologized to his girlfriend for forcing intercourse on her: 'I didn't intend to hurt or insult you. I thought all girls wanted it. Why didn't you tell me Christians behave differently? I never knew!'[3]

How can the non-Christian know? The Bible's teaching about extra-marital genital involvement is not taught today. In schools and colleges it has been replaced by more liberal views. In most churches it finds no place in the teaching curriculum. While the church remains silent, almost every pop song churns out the same persuasive, sensuous message: so long as you love one another there's no need to wait. While the church remains silent, films and plays and books and magazines propagate the same message: so long as you love one another, any form of genital intimacy is legitimate. While the church remains silent, students and nurses at the beginning of their training are advised by their tutors to go on the pill and contraceptive machines are installed in the toilets in many universities and colleges.

The Christian going out with the non-Christian not only suffers a kind of vitamin deficiency in their relationship: lack of shared prayer, shared goals, shared beliefs, mutually agreed boundaries, but in the absence of this life-giving ingredient, they are expected to summon the superlative strength required to swim against today's sexual tide. This challenge defeats some Christian couples who *are* both wanting to serve and please Christ. Not many of us are strong enough to combat such powerful, anti-God influences on our own. That is why many Christian/non-Christian relationships result in the gradual fading of the Christian's other love-life: their love for the Lord. Unable to extricate themselves from the compromise such relationships almost always present, they slink away from God, fall to attacking the church or the pastor or other Christians and are eventually lost to the fellowship.

God wants to protect us from this self-inflicted anguish, the kind of inner tug-of-war Anna was expressing when she asked that heart-rending question: 'Isn't there *any* way I can marry Robin? I love him so much.'

And God's concern rests equally with the unbelieving partner. He wants to woo them to himself. We hinder his task when, by disobedience, we say one thing with our lips and give a totally different message with our lives. As one girl lamented recently, 'How will my ex-boyfriend ever understand what God's love is now? How *could* I have been such a lousy witness?'

The gulf

I have homed in on the sexual because, for many Christians, the heart of the problem seems to lie here. But the problem is deeper, more complex than that. When a person turns to Christ, he accepts a whole new value system: the topsy-turvy standards of the kingdom of God. This affects his attitudes, his time, his talents, what he watches and listens to, where he goes, his ambitions – every particle of his being because he knows that he is under new ownership: he has been bought with an unrepeatable price. He is no longer lord of his life. Jesus is.

To the unbeliever, such a change of lordships makes not one iota of sense. It is utter foolishness. For him, there is no apparent reason why his world should not revolve around number one, seeking pleasure, the fleeting excitements of the moment. He does not live in anticipation of the Lord's return. This is not a criticism. It is a fact.

Between the Bible-observing Christian and the unbeliever, then, lies an inevitable, and in some senses an unbridgeable, gulf; a behaviour gap. That is why Paul is adamant that the two should not try to entwine their lives. The incompatibility problem is as acute as trying to introduce darkness into a room which is floodlit.

The 'wet Christian' problem

'But all the Christians I know are so wet. I don't fancy any of them.'

It has become fashionable in certain Christian circles for girls, in particular, to voice this complaint. These girls are almost always attractive, vivacious, marriageable, longing to be married and those with strong views about the kind of men who would make suitable partners for them.

The complaint is born of pain, pride and very often selfishness. The pain stems from the anguish that they have not yet found that much-sought-after but elusive phenomenon, a life partner. The pride stems from the fact that their 'husband-wanted' short-list is dictated by worldly, not Christian, criteria: good looks, good job, good prospects, good income, easy disposition: 'he's not tall enough for one thing, he's not very good looking and he's not at all sporty. I'd be embarrassed to walk down the street with him let alone turn up at church with him.' And the selfishness? I suspect that if more of these girls concentrated on fulfilling the Lord's command to love one another as he loves us, the 'wet Christian' problem would quickly become a thing of the past. Christian people sometimes appear 'wet' because no-one has come alongside them in the crucial formative years and loved out their full potential. They therefore withdraw into themselves, panic in the presence of the opposite sex, and fail to express their creativity or to grow in maturity. Criticism, complaint and condemnation help no-one. The solution to the problem is not for Christian girls to hide behind their hands and gossip about these dreadful Christian men, at the same time looking elsewhere for close relationships across the sex barrier. That, according to Paul's teaching, is disobedience. No. The solution is more radical than that. Jesus put it this way: 'Love one another as I have loved you.' That means, within the ranks of the fellowship, recognize one another's worth, draw out one another's strengths, tease out one another's full potential so that we appear to the world and to each other, not wet but gloriously alive; a walking testimony to the creativity of God.

What to say to your friends

It will be obvious from what I have already written that, in my view, when a Christian goes out with a non-Christian this is an act of disobedience.

To the question, 'Surely Christians *should* go out with non-Christians to convert them: how else will they hear about Jesus?' I would simply ask: 'Since when has effective evangelism been born from wilful disobedience?' The Bible clearly says, 'Do not be mismated with unbelievers'. True evangelism is not just *telling* people about Jesus but *leading* people into a personal relationship with Jesus. A relationship with Jesus involves us in a life of obedience: ' "Why do you call me, 'Lord, Lord,' and do not do what I say?" ' (Luke 6:46). Clearly then these lop-sided relationships cannot be designed by God as tools for evangelism.

Having taken that hard line, I would now put in a plea for a generosity of spirit amongst Christians. It very often happens that if a Christian so much as smiles at a non-Christian of the opposite sex at a party, that Christian is ostracized by the entire fellowship: shunned as though they carried some deadly disease. The Christian might start going out with a non-Christian and pluck up courage to bring their friend to church or even a Bible study. But the embarrassment and unspoken disapproval exude a lack of welcome and it is not long before the couple cease to darken Christian doors. As one of our parishioners once told me, 'I know I shouldn't have gone out with Jim when he wasn't a Christian. And I know it was disobedient to marry him. But when I did come back to the Lord, people's hard attitude made it really hard for me to return to church again.'

Chua Wee Hian, in his book, *Lovers for Life*, tells the story of a mixed marriage which once took place in Malaysia. Just before the wedding, an 'order' was passed around the church refusing Christians permission to attend. As a result, most of the tables at the wedding banquet were empty, food was wasted, the couple's confidence in their so-called friends was shattered.

Chua Wee Hian concludes, and I agree with him, 'Our concern. . .will be better expressed in other ways.'[4]

How? The most effective way to bring about any change and to dislodge any disobedience is prayer. Instead of spending valuable time gossiping about the person's backsliding, covenant to pray for them, on your own or with another person who expresses equal concern. Let this prayer spring, not from a judgmental or critical spirit (finger-pointing and compassionate prayer cannot co-exist), but let it be an expression of the love and compassion you feel for the person.

Don't nag. Don't condemn. Reflect on areas in your own life God is wanting to deal with. Keep the whole problem in perspective. And be interested in the friendship. It very often happens that a Christian going out with a non-Christian is so cold-shouldered by the Christian friends whose shock is communicated in one way or another that they have to turn to non-Christian friends to share the euphoria and the pain of the friendship. That is not just a pity but a tragedy. It is a tragedy because, even when we are being wilfully disobedient, most of us *want* to find the steep pathway which leads us back to a joy-filled relationship with God. Most of us are not strong enough or wise enough to find the way alone. Most of us need at least one Christian friend who will stand by us, love us through our waywardness, understand our rebellion, pray and support to the bitter end, until we have said our 'No' to temptation and our 'Yes' to God. And such costly friendship is what you and I are called to give. Even if the Christian decides to choose a mixed marriage, our responsibility under God is to offer support and ongoing care, not to cast the first stone.

I am not saying that we shouldn't ask concerned questions. 'What's so good about the relationship?' 'How do you feel about the absence of spiritual compatibility?' I am saying, let any such questions be conceived in the womb of love, let them be prompted by the Holy Spirit. Never quiz a person from malice, the desire to make them look small, or with the aim of cornering them so that they have no option but to fight.

What do I do next?

And if you are reading this chapter because you yourself have formed a close one-to-one relationship with an unbeliever, what must you do? If you are under eighteen and the chances of this relationship resulting in marriage are slight, weigh carefully what I have said in this chapter about mismating, weigh carefully the thesis of this book: that close one-to-one relationships have as their main purpose, the growth of the whole person: emotional, spiritual, sexual. Be honest. Is this relationship helping your spiritual growth or hindering it? If it is hindering your relationship with God, meditate on Hebrews 12:1, 'So then let us rid ourselves of everything that gets in the way, and of the sin which holds on to us so tightly, and let us run with determination the race that lies before us. Let us keep our eyes fixed on Jesus. . .'(GNB). Act appropriately.

If you are over eighteen it is possible that this relationship could result in marriage. It could be that marriage is in your partner's mind even though you may not yet seriously entertain the idea. Is it responsible Christian loving to develop a close relationship with someone you know, under God, you cannot marry? Is it responsible to allow the friendship to deepen only to pull out at the eleventh hour, with all the hurt and turmoil that entails? Is it even responsible to dilly-dally, stringing someone along in the hope that they might become a Christian? Surely not. That is not loving another, it is loving yourself.

My writing of this chapter was interrupted by an all-day Ladies Conference where I addressed two hundred women on the subject of Christian marriage. A question-box collected questions that were to be dealt with towards the close of the conference. The first question I found in that box asked: 'How can you make a Christian marriage if your husband is not a Christian?'

The short answer to that is, 'You can't'. Neither can you create the radical relationship I am describing in this book unless your partner is going the same way as you are – with Christ.

Is there any alternative at the going out stage, then, to the dreaded one: splitting up? I think not. To that painful alternative, we address ourselves in the next chapter.

Notes for chapter seven

1. W.C.G. Proctor, writing in *The New Bible Commentary* (IVP, 1953), p.995.
2. C.S. Lewis, *The Four Loves* (Collins, 1963), p.62.
3. 'Whose Responsibility?', an article published in *Sex Education* by the National Council of Women in Great Britain and quoted in the *Daily Mail* in May 1984.
4. Chong Kwong Tek and Chua Wee Hian, *Lovers for Life* (The Way Press, 1971), p.36.

8
Splitting Up

When a person you love is phased out of your life, for whatever reason, when a friendship is amputated, for whatever reason, the experience can plunge you into terrifying darkness, the nearly-drowning terror the Psalmist describes, 'All your waves and breakers have swept over me' (Psalm 42:7).

For one thing, there's the apparently interminable inner pain. Like a constant whiplash which no hand restrains, it cuts into your flesh until you are beside yourself with the horror of the pain. At the same time you might be consumed with anger: 'I've done all this for him and he just abandons me.' And there's the stunned disbelief: 'How could she just ditch me like that after all we've shared in the past?' Then there's the dread: the lasting anguish of being alone again. As one young man expressed it to me: 'The worst thing is not having anyone to belong to. That feels strange after all those months of being together.' Or as a widow once put it, 'The worst thing is having no-one to nudge. You know. I'm looking in a shop window or riding in the bus or watching television. I point to something, even start to say, "Look!" And he's not there. Then I realize he's gone. He's not going to be there.'

'He's gone. She's gone.' Such realization, such absence, such emptiness, has to be taken seriously. It can carry untold pain. It is accompanied, very often, by incessant weeping. It may even come with heart-dulling fear: 'Supposing it will always be like this? Supposing I'm unlovable?'

Is this sorrow inevitable, profitable, or is it wallowing in self-pity? How are you supposed to react to an unwanted ending to a relationship you're appreciating? Is there a way to soften the blow when the decision is not mutual but one way? *When* should we call it a day? Is it possible to revert to a platonic relationship afterwards?

In this chapter, we must centre our thoughts on such questions. How we react to such severance of friendships is of great importance. It tips the balance between an experience of utter desolation or one of prolific spiritual growth and an increase in freedom.

Is sorrow wrong?

'When my girlfriend and I split up, we both went through a terrible low patch. Is there a right and righteous and profitable side to sadness or is anything like that just wallowing in self-pity?'

Someone asked me that question at a Christian Union meeting on one occasion. I was grateful the subject of post-relationship blues had been raised. It is an important one which is not often aired.

What happens when a really close relationship breaks up, is exactly the same process people suffer when a loved one dies. At first you feel stunned. You can't take it in. You look at life as though you were seeing it through double-glazed windows or from an aeroplane. You are aware that it is happening but, although life goes on as normal, it seems to bear little relevance to you. This is the stage when your feelings are deep-frozen; when you can stare at a beautiful view yet not see it, when a blackbird can be singing in the trees outside your window, but you are incapable of hearing it. It is the phase when any form of beauty passes you by.

These feelings eventually thaw out. The tears might then flow fast and freely. It is important that you allow them to do so. They are a language. They are expressing feelings so deep that they cannot be summed up in words. Even if you are a man, weep. To cry is not unmanly or un-Christlike. 'Jesus wept' (John 11:35). It is simply un-English but that is relatively unimportant.

'Grief-work', as this process is called by psychologists,

almost always includes not only tears, but anger. The person whose loved one has died will find someone to blame: 'If only I hadn't asked him to pop down to the shops, it wouldn't have happened.' 'If only the doctor had come five minutes earlier he might have got her to hospital in time.'

The same principle applies when friends let us down. We find someone to blame. It might be ourselves. 'I must have been blind. Why didn't I realize before that he was like this? Why haven't I taken note of the trail of hurt he's caused – always making excuses, not keeping his promises.' Or it might be the other person. 'He's so selfish. He doesn't deserve a girlfriend. He only thinks about himself. He wants me when it suits him and that's all.' It might even be a third person. 'She's been trying to get him for weeks. Now he's hooked.'

Then there's the pining and the searching. When a loved one dies, this can be agonizing because, however hard you search, the loved one cannot be found. But when the loved one is only a telephone call away, the temptation is to pick up the 'phone and to make contact. That is why a couple whose relationship is dying will often drive their friends crazy. One day the relationship is off, the following weekend it is on again. This yo-yo relationship might continue, up and down, up and down for weeks, even months, before it finally fizzles out.

These painful grief procedures must be worked through; the pain must not be repressed. Repress it and it will pop up again in a disguised form a few months later. Work through it, like a tug-boat plodding its way upstream, and you will find a miracle taking place however slowly and gradually. You will nose your way into unexplored and exhilarating freedoms; you can have a new and deep relationship with Christ.

Therefore, to feel stunned for a while, a part of the world yet strangely distant from it, is not wallowing in self-pity, it is normal. Weeping is not necessarily wallowing in self-pity. This soggy stage, too, is normal, therapeutic. To pine and search is not wallowing in self-pity. It is normal. Even being angry is not necessarily wallowing in self-pity. It is also normal, although, as Christians, we have to learn that difficult art of being angry but not falling into sin (Ephesians 4:26).

You cross the fingernail-thin border between grief and self-pity when you allow this all-consuming sadness to fill your horizon to the exclusion of everything else. You cross over from grief to self-pity when you refuse to pass on from these initial stages of loss to the next, essential stages: where you deliberately detach yourself from the loved one, where you forgive yourself and the loved one for any mistakes which have been made or any hurts inflicted, and where, last of all, you wave goodbye to the loved one, to the relationship as it was and the relationship as it might have been, and you uncurl your hands, a sign, as it were, that you are ready to receive from God whatever he chooses to give you in place of this partner.

These later stages, of course, do not happen all at once. They come gradually. They may take months rather than weeks. They come through prayer. They come through trust. But as they come, they can bring a priceless gift with them: a deeper relationship with Christ.

A new love-relationship
This, at least, was my experience on one occasion. When I was an undergraduate, I fell in love with a fellow member of the committee of the Christian Union. He was the president, I was the secretary. For months I loved from afar. Then I plucked up courage to allow my feelings to be known. Our relationship deepened as the months passed. But when, one cold November day, he told me that 'it was not God's will' for us to go out together, I was devastated.

My room-mate's listening ear brought one form of comfort. But the disappointment and humiliation and sense of loss ran so deep that human words and human hands could find no access to the root of the pain. It was then that I discovered for the first time that aloneness need not spell loneliness; it can mature into that lovely thing called solitude.

I remember studying the Song of Solomon at that time and

being stirred by God's bridegroom-love. I remember his gentle in-breathing, his tender touching of those grazed and bruised places deep within. Although that crisis erupted nearly thirty years ago, I look back on it as one of the lasting landmarks of my spiritual growth. In my lostness, God found me. And to be found by him is special.

He has not changed. I am watching similar growth take place in a very attractive young friend of mine at the moment. Her relationship with her boyfriend broke up recently. She was stunned. She cried, she was angry, she was tempted to pick up the 'phone just to hear his voice once more. But every week, it seems, she gives me a fresh bulletin. 'Joyce! The Lord is being so good. First he showed me how selfish I am – then he seemed to go out of his way to show me, just in little ways, how much he loves me. Now he's giving me such a close relationship with himself. Prayer is terrific.'

How can we soften the blow?

Even so, when the decision to end a relationship is a one-way decision, the blow could cause deep and lasting pain: the horrendous pain of abandonment, the crippling pain of rejection, and the dull, persistent ache I described at the beginning of this chapter. If we are to fulfil the law of Christ and love our partner as we love ourselves we must cushion them as much as possible.

Part of this cushioning will be done apart from the partner by praying for them, before, throughout and after the break-up. Part of it will be done, not by what you say, but by the way you say it. Communication experts assure us that the words we use make up a mere 7% of the message we convey while the tone of voice contributes 38% of the message. The other 55% consists of non-verbal communication: the expression on our face, the look in our eyes, the appropriateness of our touch, the genuineness of our concern. And part of the cushioning will come through the reasons you give for pulling out of the friendship at this moment in time.

If you want to pull out because you are attracted to someone else, you must say so. If you want to pull out because the partnership no longer provides a springboard for serving God, you must say so. If you want to pull out because you are no longer able to give your partner the kind of love which is essential where both partners are to grow, you must say so. But in saying so, if you are to soften the blow, it is important that you accept full responsibility for your feelings. As Selwyn Hughes rightly observes, 'Speaking the truth in love means using the truth as observation and not as accusation.'[1] In other words, in this situation you would refrain from over-spiritualizing in a woolly way, 'I don't believe God wants us to go out together any more.' You would refrain from accusing, 'You're dragging me down spiritually.' Instead, you might say something like, 'I know it's going to be hard for you to hear this. I know it could feel as though I'm rejecting you. I'm not fed up with you, nor do I want to reject you, but I'm finding myself unable to give to you and our relationship in the way I used to. It's probably me, but I find I'm further away from God than I used to be and the relationship doesn't seem to be helping. . . .'

Of course it would not come out pat like that. You can't rehearse such a speech and make it genuine. But you can get the point: don't blame, don't accuse, don't compound the problem by lashing out or bringing up past mistakes. Accept your uncertainties as yours, express them as yours and be gentle, loving, yet decisive.

When?

And, of course, the timing is often crucial. 'I sometimes wonder what God thinks about our relationship. I sometimes ask him but he doesn't seem to say anything. So I don't know whether I should stop going out with my boyfriend or not. If I do, when? And what reason should I give?'

The girl who made that observation to me was going out with an unbeliever and God had clearly been convicting her for several months already that certain changes in the relationship were long overdue.

When, like this sincere young Christian, we ask God a direct question like: 'What do you want me to do about this friendship?', three things are necessary. First, we must be honest enough to ask ourselves the question, 'Do I really trust God?' Second, we must be brave enough to face the question, 'Am I really willing to hear what he says, to be guided by him?' Third, we must be self-aware enough to confront the challenge, 'Am I prepared to hear his answer?' If we can say 'Yes' to each of these questions, then we must search or wait for God's answer.

I say 'search' first because one of the antennae God has given us is the mind and we must use our minds to discover what God's revealed Word, the Bible, has to say in reply to our question. We might find the question does not require a writing-on-the-wall or God-speaking-in-a-dream reply because the reply is there in front of us in black and white in the pages of the Bible.

For example, the girl I have already mentioned had been going out with an unbeliever for nearly two years. They had indulged in sexual intercourse on several occasions. She admitted that if they continued to go out together, she would be unable to resist the temptation to repeat the sexual sin; she was not even certain that she wanted to resist.

What does God's word *say* about such relationships? Psalm 1:1 puts the situation in a nutshell. 'Happy the man who never follows the advice of the wicked, or loiters on the way that sinners take' (JB). Paul puts it even more succinctly: 'Do not harness yourselves . . . with unbelievers' (2 Corinthians 6:14 JB) The pen-picture Paul paints is powerful. Harness yourself with an unbeliever and you create an uneven team. The picture is of a mature ox yoked to an immature one. Both partners of the pair suffer chafing to the shoulders because of the unequalness of the pairing. Just as oxen need to be carefully and evenly matched, so do we.

If you are going out with an unbeliever and you also want to live biblically, you have to apply the following questions to the Bible passages we looked at earlier: Are you prepared to listen to God? Are you prepared to be guided by God? Are you prepared to trust God with your entire future?

'I don't think I could give my boyfriend up even if God asked me to. We'd split for a couple of days, then we'd be back together again. I like him that much.'

The speaker was the same girl I mentioned earlier, the one

with the non-Christian boyfriend. Although her lip-prayers
asked God the question: 'What do you think of this relationship?', her heart-prayer dictated the answer: 'Please don't
ask me to give him up. At least, not yet.'

The cost of commitment

Why? Why are we so reluctant to hold any relationship on
the open palm of our hand? Why do we tighten our fists
around relationships so that God himself cannot prise the
person from our tightly clenched knuckles? The reason is
that we are less committed to Christ than we think we are.

In his powerful little book, *The Cost of Commitment*, John
White reproduces a challenging letter written by an
unknown American communist to his fiancée. The letter was
an attempt to explain why he was breaking off their
engagement.

> We communists suffer many casualties. We are those
> whom they shoot, hang, lynch, tar and feather, imprison,
> slander, fire from our jobs and whose lives people make
> miserable in every way possible. Some of us are killed and
> imprisoned. We live in poverty. From what we earn we
> turn over to the Party every cent which we do not ab-
> solutely need to live. . . .
>
> There is one thing about which I am completely in
> earnest – the communist cause. It is my life, my business,
> my religion, my hobby, my sweetheart, my wife, my mis-
> tress, my meat and drink. I work at it by day and dream of
> it by night. Its control over me grows greater with the
> passage of time. Therefore I cannot have a friend, a lover
> or even a conversation without relating them to this power
> that animates and controls my life. I measure people,
> books, ideas and deeds according to the way they affect the
> communist cause and by their attitude to it. I have already
> been in jail for my ideas, and if need be I am ready to face
> death.[2]

For this American, communism was his treasure – the pearl
for which it was worth abandoning everything.

Jesus said, '*The kingdom of heaven* is like treasure hidden in a field. When a man found it, he hid it again, and then *in his joy* went and sold all he had and bought that field' (Matthew 13:44, italics mine). The implication here is clear: commitment to Jesus should so grab us that we long to offer him the kind of total devotion which motivated this communist's life and choices.

The seemingly reckless man in the parable, like the communist, stood still, took stock and acted accordingly. They both re-evaluated their priorities. In the light of their number one priority, they reshaped their lives. And, as Christians, we are called to make that same degree of commitment: love for Jesus (which means obeying Jesus) is our life-goal. Everything else either falls into place under the King's shadow or must be shed if it is incompatible with the life of the kingdom. We cannot cling to treasures of the old life and, at the same time, hold up eager, cup-open hands to receive the treasures of the kingdom. There is not room for both.

When two Christians part
But maybe you have been going out not with a non-Christian but with a fellow believer? Maybe your relationship used to be good for both of you? Maybe it has grown stale? Or you have become inward looking? Maybe you feel uneasy for other reasons?

If you accept my thesis, that such relationships exist for the support of both partners and to further the emotional and spiritual, the sexual and relational growth of the fellow and the girl, it follows that when the relationship seems to have outgrown this function, this will be the autumn of the friendship. Autumn inevitably leads to winter.

That is not to say that either partner should be tossed into the toy cupboard like a discarded, once-loved teddy-bear. It is to say that the time has come for the couple to recognize that the need for change exists, at least for one partner; that this change is inevitable and must be effected as gently, as lovingly, as painlessly and as quickly as possible. Long-drawn-out partings are the most agonizing: they do nothing to diminish or eliminate the inevitable anguish. They increase the desolation of the partner who continues to cling.

If you know the curtain fall is coming, therefore, be decisive. Finality is, in fact, kinder than dilly-dallying. 'When Jonathan came round and told me it was all over, that he was, in fact, attracted to someone else, I knew that was it. It was senseless to hope any more. He meant it. I could tell. I wept buckets and I'm afraid I was very angry but in a funny way, it helped me. I knew I had to get over it. I knew I had to get over him.'

Getting over it

How do you get over it? How do you ensure this becomes a rich period of your life? How do you re-establish a platonic relationship with your partner? We must move on to look at these pertinent questions.

I sometimes wish that Christian fellowships would become more acutely aware of the needs of those in the painful transition period under scrutiny. Their role in the life of the Christian at this stage is vital. Their contribution could even tip the make-or-break balance.

There is absolutely no point in telling someone who has just 'lost' their boyfriend or girlfriend to snap out of it. This they cannot do. Neither will they necessarily find themselves consoled by or helped by Bible reading, fellowship meetings or prayer at first. During the initial shocked phase I described, nothing penetrates. The role of the fellowship, then, is not to nag, not to condemn, not to criticize, not even to advise, but simply to love sensitively and to pray the person through the tunnel; to go on praying until they have struggled to the sunlit mouth at the tunnel's furthest end.

If you are in the position of loss yourself, although it may be hard to admit you need help, ask a few trusted friends to pray for you Knowing that they are doing so will release you from pressure and may well result in a much faster, more effective recovery.

Making it a spiritually rich time

At the same time, there are things you can do to help yourself avoid the snare of self-pity and to ensure that this becomes, for you, a spiritual landmark.

First, make a clean breast of any mistakes you made in the relationship which leave you with a stain on your conscience or with pangs of regret. Second, forgive yourself and your partner. (For suggestions of ways to do this, see the last chapter of this book.) Third, recognize that there are three things you can do with the anger which flares inside you: fight the flames, run away from them, or switch off the gas. In this situation the healthiest way to cope with the anger is to recognize that there is little, if anything, that can be done about it now. Therefore, switch off the gas by handing the anger to God, let him sift it, extract what is sinful and receive back from him only what is righteous anger. Relax. And fourth, trust. In other words, acknowledge that your life and the whole of your future lie, in C.S. Lewis's memorable phrase, 'between the paws of Aslan', in other words safely in the hands of the Lord who rules the universe. Fifth, make a list of the good things which the relationship gave you and thank God for them. Sixth, drop your anchor back into the haven of God's presence. And rest.

You might find a version of the following prayer will help you over the hump.

'Lord Jesus Christ, you see me just as I am. Thank you that I do not have to hide my brokenness from you. You see the bruises and the scars. Thank you that your hands will touch and soothe them with gentleness and love.

'Lord, you know how I failed you in this friendship. The memory of _____ burdens me. Please forgive me for _____ and forgive my partner for _____. I give to you my pain and my anger. Sift the anger, Lord. Take away what is stained with sin and hand back to me only the anger which is righteous indignation. May I gradually turn my back on what might have been. Would you illuminate this present darkness with yourself. Relight the flame of trust in me. I want to trust you for my future. I want to discover you in the middle of the present turmoil. Even more, in my lostness, I want to be found by you. Thank you for all that

you gave me through this relationship; for _____
and _____ and _____ . May I, streng-
thened by these gifts of love, enrich the lives of others, even
meet them in their need even if I am only one of your
wounded healers. The little craft of my life seems very
storm-tossed at the moment. The sea of life seems so big.
May I drop anchor in the harbour-calm of your love. May
I be filled with your peace. For the glory of Jesus. Amen.'

A prayer like that could be the beginning of many new
beginnings, particularly the beginning of an ever-deepening
friendship with God, a subject we shall return to in the next
chapter.

As well as reaching out for help from others and consola-
tion in God, I have two other self-help suggestions to make.
First, do not neglect Christian fellowship. Second, rediscover
the delights of being unattached to one particular person.

Christian fellowship

When two people in love allow the roots of their lives to
intertwine, the relationship can consume huge slices of time.
It often happens that such couples cut themselves off from
the fellowship. We realize how unwise we have been only
when the relationship ends and we find ourselves like a
dislocated arm hanging loose from its socket.

The wise thing to do is to slot ourselves back into our
rightful place so that we can function normally again.
Although this is wise, we often resist it. Pride is one reason.
Fear is another. Spiritual apathy is a third. We fear to return
after weeks, maybe months, of absence. Even if we do return,
we may find ourselves critical of the set-up because it does
not seem to meet our immediate need. The problem here,
which we must come to terms with, is that nothing and
no-one will meet our apparent need. What we think we need
is so often confused with what we want. We probably want
one thing only: the return of the relationship. In the absence
of this we feel empty. The fellowship will never be a substitute. But it can offer a supportive ministry, and that is
what we really do need at this moment in time.

Enjoy your freedom

As we discover this for ourselves, so, too, we can rediscover the perks of being unattached to a particular person. There are some. Indeed, there are plenty! As one young man put it, 'It's strange. I miss her. But I'm quite enjoying being free again. It's quite good to be unattached.'

The unattached person enjoys complete freedom of movement, freedom of choice, freedom of friends. Enjoy all these to the full. Use the opportunity to make new friends. In particular, enjoy the stimulus of group friendships, going to concerts with several people, relaxing with a mixed party of people, using your flat or bed-sit or college room as a base for entertaining a vast variety of acquaintances, or for drawing alongside others in need.

Margaret Evening, in her classic book on singleness, tells of an occasion when she did just this:

One extremely cold winter's afternoon, I lit a roaring fire in my lovely Cornish-stone fireplace, drew up a settee, plumped up the cushions, put my feet up and settled back for a cosy afternoon with a box of chocolates and a novel, with Polycarp (my cat) wrapped round my feet. The novel was *The Dean's Watch* by Elizabeth Goudge. I read of Mary Montague who was crippled by a fall as a child. In her dreams she planned a life full of adventures, but gradually as she grew up she realised that never would she embark on those adventures, and her chances of marriage were almost non-existent.

With no prospects of a career or marriage it seemed that she was doomed to life-long boredom, but then in a moment of awakening, it dawned upon her that *loving* could be a vocation in itself, a life work. It could be a career, like marriage or nursing, or going on stage. Loving could be an adventure. Firstly, she accepted the vocation and took a vow to love.

God spoke to me through Mary Montague that afternoon. . . .I suddenly saw how my loving had been lacking in energy because I had been harbouring resentment (against God, I suppose) that I hadn't a husband and

children . . . .Staring at the fire, I prayed to be delivered
from the bondage of my own yearnings and longings and
to be gloriously freed from the feverish desires that could
block the path of such a vocation . . . .I put the novel on
one side. . . and went to fetch a young colleague who lived
in a dingy bed-sit. I found her huddled over the one bar of
a totally inadequate electric fire, still wearing the anorak
that she had put on that morning whilst the room 'warmed
up'. She came home with me and together we toasted our
toes in front of the fire and talked into the night. For both
of us there was far more warmth in that weekend than
came from the fire blazing in the hearth.[3]

That kind of friendship requires, not skill, but courage and
overflowing love.

If you are musical, make music. Music is not only a
ministry to those who listen, its unique ministry percolates
deep down to touch the unexpressed, often unacknowledged
needs of those to whom the gift has been entrusted. If you
stop to think about it, this makes a great deal of sense. Music
is about harmonization. When we make harmony, when we
replace fragmentation with integration, we make peace,
'shalom', peace as Jesus gives it.

Even if you cannot make music, you can create beauty.
God is a God who delights to garnish his world with loveli-
ness, to bring order out of chaos, a well-watered garden from
the howling wilderness. In small, but significant ways, we
can become imitators of him. In our home, for example, even
where this is one room in someone else's house or in a nurses'
home or hall of residence, by using our imagination we can
introduce simple, but striking, breath-catching splendour: a
perfect pine cone collected from the woods, a single flower in
a vase, a particular poster which points Godwards. Embel-
lishing your 'pad' in this way does something to the 'inner
you'. It motivates you to live for today, to live fully and
creatively in the present, to refuse to fritter away God's
precious gift of the here-and-now by indulging in useless
daydreams.

Was this why Betsie Ten Boom transformed the con-

demned cell where she lived with a number of other women?
Corrie Ten Boom, Betsie's famous sister, records:

> This cell was charming. . . .The straw pallets were rolled
> instead of piled in a heap, standing like pillars along the
> walls, each with a lady's hat atop it. A headscarf had
> somehow been hung along the wall. The contents of
> several food packages were arranged on a small
> shelf. . . .Even the coats hanging on their hooks were part
> of the welcome of that room, each sleeve draped over the
> shoulder of the coat next to it like a row of dancing
> children.[4]

If you find yourself unattached after many months of being
attached, make friends, make music, make beauty. And
determine, with an act of the will, to make the most of this
no-man's-land, if such it proves to be.

There are things you can accomplish without a partner
which you cannot do so easily with a partner in tow I was
amused to read Barbara Cartland's recognition of this fact
recently. At 83, she still writes twenty-five lucrative, bestselling novels a year. She is supposed to have admitted to one
newspaper reporter, 'Of course, I couldn't do all this with a
husband.'

There are things we can do for Christ while we remain
single and unattached which the married person cannot do.
Adventure into these projects. Enjoy them to the full. Live
fully in the 'here and now'. Apart from the personal legacy
this will leave to you, it will bring glory to Christ. As
Irenaeus put it, 'The glory of God is a man fully alive.'

Renegotiating the friendship

And what of the friendship? Can that be renegotiated on a
new set of terms? Can it revert to a brother-sister relationship
in Christ once the romantic has evaporated or hopes of
marriage been slashed? I believe it can. But it takes time,
resilience and a great deal of grace.

Let me quote from Corrie Ten Boom's book *The Hiding
Place* again. In that book Corrie recalls the occasion when the

young man she loved and who, she believed, loved her, arrived on her doorstep with his new wife. It had not occurred to him to warn her so the shock and bewilderment left Corrie reeling. It was in the quietness of her own room that she tried to come to terms with the pain, the anguish, the confusion and the grief. How should she react? What was to happen to her love for him? How could she prevent herself from becoming angry, resentful or bitter? Questions like these plagued her.

Eventually — and it took time — she struggled to the big-heartedness where she could pray for them both, love them both, and ask God to enrich their marriage with his love.

Not many of us will be entrusted with that degree of pain. What might puzzle us is how to react when we meet our ex-boyfriend in the lift; how to react when we see our ex-girlfriend going out with someone else.

When you have let go of the friendship as it might have been, if both agree that friendship within a low-key framework is beneficial to you both, it *is* possible to meet in a group situation to laugh, to learn, and even to have fun again. But it takes time, as I said, and the determination to break through the embarrassment, to allow the past to be past and to enjoy all that the present friendship offers.

'It takes time.' The no-man's-land between the relationship as it was and the friendship which might emerge from the ashes can be a lonely time. Loneliness must therefore move to the foreground of our minds in the next chapter.

Notes for chapter eight

1. Selwyn Hughes, *Marriage as God Intended* (Kingsway, 1983), p.56.
2. John White, *The cost of commitment* (IVP, 1976), pp.52–53.
3. Margaret Evening, *Who Walk Alone* (Hodder and Stoughton, 1974), pp.200–201.
4. Corrie Ten Boom, *The Hiding Place*, quoted in *Who Walk Alone* by Margaret Evening, pp.184–185.

9
Loneliness:
A Friend in Disguise

You don't have to be jilted to experience loneliness. But if you are jilted, as we saw in the last chapter, you experience loneliness as a physical and psychic pain. It leaves you exhausted, despairing of life, yourself, others and maybe of God also.

You don't have to be a teenager to experience loneliness. But adolescence and young adulthood, as everyone knows, are the notorious peak periods when loneliness invades the spirit as surreptitiously as a deadly disease enters the bloodstream. This malignancy seems to thrive inside you, but it saps your energy, paralyses you and leaves you crippled with fear: the fear of becoming a fringe person instead of one of the 'in crowd'; the fear of taking the risk of giving yourself to others or of receiving any of the warmth they offer; above all, the fear that the real you does not matter to anyone: that you do not have access to the personal resources to 'make it' into adulthood.

Graham Kendrick puts the germ of this dread in a heart-rending song:

> Scared to be weak, scared to be strong
> Scared to be right and scared to be wrong
> Scared to death, scared of life
> Scared to run, scared to fight
> Scared the world might find out what you're like
> For you doubt if they'd love you for just who you are
> Oh does anybody love you for just who you are?. . .

Scared to be you, scared to be loved
Acting the part and frightened to stop
For you doubt if they'd love you for just who you are
Oh does anybody love you for just who you are?. . .

Scared to believe, frightened to doubt
Scared to come in and scared to stay out
For you doubt if they'd love you for just who you are,
Oh does anybody love you for just who you are?

(Breaking of the Dawn)

You don't have to be young to be lonely. You can be becalmed by loneliness at any stage of your life, during any phase of your career. Loneliness assaults rich and poor alike, young and old alike, drop-outs and high-fliers alike. But loneliness, as I said, attaches itself like a shadow to the under thirties, and particularly to people falling in and out of love. That is why I propose to devote a whole chapter to loneliness.

The condition called loneliness gives rise to certain questions: What is loneliness? Why do we feel lonely? What can we do when it takes the wind out of our sails? Why does this chapter heading claim it is a friend in disguise?

What is loneliness?

When we understand a certain phenomenon, it helps us to handle it. The first thing we must do, therefore, is to clarify what loneliness is and what it is not.

Billy Graham calls loneliness a problem. In fact, he claims that loneliness is the greatest problem facing mankind today. Mother Teresa of Calcutta also sees it as a heart-hunger and claims that it is easier to relieve material poverty than this poverty of the soul. Jesus experienced loneliness as a weight, a whole load of sorrow to be shifted. In Gethsemane, as we shall see later, he demonstrates how this sorrow can be disposed of.

It sometimes seems as though successful people are more susceptible to loneliness than others. Albert Einstein is supposed to have written to a friend on one occasion, 'It is strange to be known so universally and yet to be so lonely.' Joan Crawford, the film actress, ended her own life: 'Lonely, bitter, reclusive', the newspaper story described her. When Barbara Hutton, the multi-millionairess, died, the news-papers announced her death with this headline: 'Hutton spent life fleeing from loneliness'.[1]

Christian executives and entertainers, writers and preachers, do not escape this same feeling of loneliness. Monday mornings, for example, frequently brought with them the sting of loneliness for the great preacher, Charles Spurgeon. Martin Luther, it is said, often sobbed himself to sleep like a great child. More recently, David Watson, in his bestselling book *You are My God,* makes no secret of the fact that success, even in a Christian context, brings its own strand of loneliness. Loneliness is the gulf between who you are and who others think you are. It is the gap between what you can realistically do under God and what others expect of you. Loneliness is sitting on a pedestal surrounded by adulating admirers; alone.

Loneliness is a feeling: or, more accurately, a jumble of feelings. It is the feeling that you matter to people, not for who you are, but for what you can do. For some, it goes deeper than that: it is the anxiety that you do not matter at all. If you died tomorrow, no-one would even notice, let alone care. It is a feeling of alienation. It is a feeling of being cut off by others. It is feeling that no-one is even aware of your heart-hunger, *your* need for care, love and support. Loneliness comes through loss, through displacement: the feeling that you have ceased to be important to a particular person or body of people. Loneliness attacks the senses so that you feel isolated from your peers. You seem to be rejected, estranged, abandoned, you believe that nowhere are you fully understood.

We must not ignore this bleak side of the two-sided coin of loneliness. But neither must we forget to flip the coin over; to examine its other face. If we do neglect the friendly face of loneliness, we become self-pitying bores, we lose our attrac-tiveness, we may even lose the few friends we do have.

The friendly faces of loneliness

I do not write that observation lightly. As I write this chapter I am just emerging from a particularly painful phase of loneliness. A month ago I caught a mysterious virus. It seemed to drain me of my last ounce of energy and forced me to spend hours on my own. In retrospect, I am glad because it means that what I write here about the friendly face of loneliness is born from the immediacy of experience. Far from being glib or distanced, though I fear that anything *written* about loneliness does read that way, it is born from the authenticity of the recent, bitter-sweet experience.

One lesson I have learned during this fallow time is that loneliness is a language which, like all languages, is capable of conveying messages. The message loneliness wants to etch on our hearts is the message which runs through this entire book. We need to be loved. We need the love of friends. We need the love of God.

I know this is obvious, but just as we take green fields and white lilac for granted until we move from the countryside into a flat in the city's concrete jungle, so we take love for granted until an emptiness yawns somewhere deep down inside us. That gaping inner emptiness can be one of the friendly faces of loneliness if we will listen to its message: Your need for love is urgent.

Most of us work hard at papering over the cracks caused by loneliness. We over-work to beguile the world and ourselves into believing that all is well. We flit from one superficial social engagement to another to give the impression that we are popular, though deep down we know that this is compounding the loneliness problem, not solving it. We clutter ourselves with spiritual paraphernalia and rush from this service to that rally, from this Bible study to that prayer meeting in an attempt to present to the watching world an image which, alas, does not stand the test of time. And the inner bleep of loneliness refuses to be silenced. It brings us face to face with reality: not the personal success-story we project to the world, but the true situation: our inner poverty. Thus loneliness is the friend in disguise who brings us face to face with the truth: Your loneliness is a breakdown of trust. You have been neglecting to trust God for the present; failing to place your future in his care.

Loneliness sometimes behaves like a friendly wind. It demolishes the fences we erect when we attempt to live self-sufficient lives. It leaves us exposed, not to inflict on us more hurt but to provide an access through which healing and hope may enter.

Why do we feel lonely?

This pathway to healing must always be kept clear because, important as friends are to our well-being, the day will almost certainly come when they let us down; when those who *say* we matter to them fail to detect our need; when even those closest to us seem too preoccupied with their own affairs to stand alongside us in a time of blackness or despair. On such occasions loneliness can take on terrifying proportions. Jesus experienced the horror of this kind of loneliness and he showed us how to deal with it.

Think for a moment of the events immediately preceding Jesus' anguish in Gethsemane. He has dined with his twelve companions for the last time. He has walked with them through the cypress groves. He has unburdened his soul to his three closest friends, confessing, 'The sorrow in my heart is so great that it almost crushes me' (Mark 14:34 GNB). He has begged for their support and care. 'Stay here and keep watch' (Mark 14:34 GNB). And the disciples fall asleep.

But Jesus does not rail at the fickleness of friends, nor lament that even the richest friendships are fragile. Instead he turns to *the* Friend, his Father. In his Father's presence he finds peace, strength and the courage to go on.

Peace, *shalom,* means, among other things, joy in God, being in tune with him, and rooted in his unfailing love. Jesus triumphed over loneliness by dropping anchor into the haven of God's presence. Just as he did this at the height of his loneliness, in the Garden of Gethsemane, we must learn to do the same at all times. This is what turns the trauma of *loneliness* into the bliss of *solitude.*

In other words, like Jesus, we must cultivate an accurate awareness of the inestimable value of friends without exalting the gift of human friendship. We must hold in tension the twin realizations: that human friendship does offer healing but that on this alone we must not depend. Our dependency must rest on God.

What this means in practice, I believe, is that, when we find ourselves aching with loneliness, maybe even bursting into tears at odd times of the day and for no apparent reason, too fearful to pick up the 'phone to talk to a friend, instead of being persuaded that nobody cares, we creep into the refuge of the presence of God. In that place of tested security, we expose our fear, give voice to our inability to cope with the disappointment life offers day after day and stay there until it is no longer me revealing my emptiness to God, but rather God who reveals his supportive love to me.

I do not know who 'Elizabeth' is. What I do know is that 'Elizabeth' has experienced just what I am trying to describe. She has expressed it in a poem which never fails to move me.

> The enshrouding blackness
> engulfs my being.
> Alone.
> Afraid.
> My mind a whirlpool
> ever inwards
> towards an eternity of intolerable pain.
>
> I used to reach out
> a hand
> into the black unknown
> in hope.
> But my soul was torn from me,
> and I hoped no more.
>
> It was like a pit.
> Unfathomable depth.
> Tortuous grovelling
> My tears the only sound
> in the impenetrable darkness.

I remember that pit,
and the fear,
and the hopelessness
of an eternal agony of mind,
and the soulless wandering
in uncharted desert.

Now I find myself at this oasis,
this unlooked-for harbour,
this refuge.
I did not deserve that gracious act
to pluck me from that all-powerful deep.

I had no hope,
but turning back along the path I came,
I see a gracious hand
and a loving smile.
I see a guiding light
and feel a protecting wing.

Nestling in your warmth
my cold heart has thawed.
The blackness of my soul
has blossomed into a million blooms.

My tears have turned to jewels,
and my bitterness to honey.

But I remember the pit.
Keep me, O Lord,
Safe
in the refuge of your wings.[2]

The Friend beyond all

It is not friendship with human friends which affords this
security. No. At some time or another, friends will fail us
because we will come lower on their list of priorities than our
pressing needs can tolerate. Our friendship with Jesus can
truly meet us in this exile. This is the other half of the

message of this book. As humans we cannot exist without love. We need the love of friends. We also need the consoling friendship of Jesus.

Thomas à Kempis put this in a memorable way:

When Jesus is present all is well and nothing seems difficult. When Jesus is absent all is hard. When Jesus does not speak within, comfort is worthless. Yet if Jesus speaks but a single word, great comfort is felt. Did not Mary. . .rise at once from the place in which she was weeping, when Martha said to her, "The Master is here and calls you?" Happy hour when Jesus calls the spirit from tears to gladness. How dry and hard you are without Jesus: how foolish and empty if you desire anything apart from Jesus. . . .To be without Jesus is a bitter underworld: and to be with Jesus, a sweet paradise. . . .

You cannot very well live without a friend, and if Jesus is not your friend beyond all, you will be exceedingly sad and lonely. . . .Therefore of all dear ones let Jesus alone be specially loved.[3]

Friendship with Jesus

Friendship with Jesus is intimacy. It is availability. And it is constancy. Jesus' offer of friendship means that we shall never, ever, be alone again. We may *feel* alone but our feelings mislead us. Jesus is at pains to assure us of this fact. Other friends may depart. He will not: ' "You will not be left all alone; I will come back to you" ' (John 14:18 GNB). 'God has said, "I will never leave you; I will never abandon you." Let us be bold, then, and say, "The Lord is my helper, I will not be afraid. What can anyone do to me?" ' (Hebrews 13:5–6 GNB). 'Does a woman forget her baby at the breast, or fail to cherish the son of her womb? Yet even if these forget, I will never forget you. See, I have branded you on the palms of my hands' (Isaiah 49:15–16 JB).

What this means, in effect, is that whenever the storm of loneliness threatens to drown us, we can place our hand in the hand of the God who dwells within: the constant, caring companion Jesus. There will never come a time when his rescue bid is not on hand. For Jesus' involvement in our lives is likened, in the New Testament, to the commitment of marriage. Jesus is the heavenly bridegroom. We are his bride. He wants us to relate to him in the confidence that his love is faithful, unending, permanent.

Amazing though that dimension of love is, perhaps the most special ingredient of Jesus' love is that in this friendship we return, not simply to a tributary of love, we return to the pure source of all love and of our own existence also. To return to this source is deeply consoling.

We see this in nature. In spring, if you walk through a field where lambs and sheep graze side by side, you will find that the very sight of a person will send the lambs scampering to their mother. They will snuggle into her, suckle and stay close to her side until the danger has passed. The friendship Jesus offers is similar though even more secure. When loneliness bears down on us, he is our hiding place. There is no safer refuge in the universe than sheltering under the shadow of his wings.

Steps out of loneliness
Since the friendship and support Jesus offers is constant, as Christians we need never be lonely. Jesus' day-and-night availability calls us from our loneliness. Even so, as I explained at the beginning of this chapter, many Christians are plagued by loneliness. It therefore seems essential further to explore how the desert of loneliness can be transformed; how aloneness can become the solitude where we are recreated.

If this is to happen, one of the first things we must do is to take the risk of responding to the love of Jesus I have just described. In practice this means exposing our loneliness to God's gaze, committing the pain of our loneliness to him and taking the leap of faith so that we land in the arms of God.

We must also reject the suggestion that *aloneness* necessarily spells *loneliness*. We do not have to suffer loneliness whenever we are by ourselves. With this realization in the forefront of our mind, we may experiment. Rather than running away from our own company, we will carve out time when, like Mary of Bethany, we can 'just be' alone with Jesus. I am not talking here about our daily times of quiet with God. I am recommending some added extras: leisure time deliberately earmarked 'Aloneness' when we seek to discover for ourselves that solitude can be creative; where we seek the realization that the space inside us is in the dwelling place of the most high God who converts man's emptiness into fullness.

If you take time to do this, you will discover that in prayer you do not simply cry, 'Help!', you will know yourself helped. You will not simply ask: you will receive. You will not simply talk. You will know yourself heard, held together and healed.[4]

Trust

God is always calling us to trust. And, as we have seen, loneliness is the failure to trust. God calls us from this form of loneliness. He asks us to fix our eyes, not on the storm within but on him. You may feel your ability to trust is no bigger than a mustard seed. Never mind. Invest that in the Bank of Heaven. Without such trust it is impossible to please him. Without such trust we become estranged from him. Without such minimal trust we never enjoy the dividends he so generously provides. And remember that true trust exists even when there seem to be no concrete reasons for hope.

Believe facts not feelings

Loneliness, as we have observed, is a *feeling:* a deep 'gut-feeling', but a feeling nevertheless. The problem with feelings is that they masquerade as facts. If I feel abandoned or rejected or estranged or isolated or cut off, therefore, I am quickly persuaded that someone somewhere has cast me on one side, rejected me or neglected me. This may or may not be true of our human friends. But it certainly is *not* true of our heavenly Friend. The fact of the matter is that we are not *totally* abandoned, no matter what our feelings may dictate to the contrary. In fact, we are uniquely loved by God. These facts must be kept in razor-sharp perspective and placed alongside the fuzziness of our feelings. We must go further and give thanks to God that these *are* facts.

When we do this, we find our pace quickening. Our hearts will be so full of gratitude, so full of God's love, that we will find ourselves capable of shedding the unrealistic and demanding expectations we had placed on others when we considered that *they* were responsible for alleviating our loneliness, that *they* held the key to our deep-seated needs being met. Gradually the realization dawns upon us that that telephone call which we hoped would come is not the full answer to our loneliness problem. Neither is that much-longed-for letter. Neither is the forging of that particular much-fancied friendship. No. These things are peripheral. The solution to the loneliness problem is found only in friendship with Jesus. Look elsewhere and you run headlong into disappointment, if not despair.

Be a good friend
I am not backtracking. I am not cancelling out the earlier chapters of this book where I emphasized our need for human friendship. I am saying that, although we need close one-to-one friendships, we also need an intimate relationship with Jesus; that certain love-needs can be met only in the divine embrace; that loneliness is the friend in disguise who throws us into the arms of Christ.

If you think about it, it makes sense. If you know yourself deeply loved by someone who will never let you down, fail you or phase out of your life, you are rich in resources. This means that you do not spend your life searching for love. You have found it. From the fullness of your inner resources, that inner space where God not only dwells but reigns, you are capable of giving to others.

Serve others
On several occasions God seems to have underlined, for me, that such self-giving is, in fact, one way out of loneliness. Two such occasions spring to mind.

The first happened several years ago when, exhausted after a draining spell of ministry in the parish, culminating in a week-end conference where loneliness struck me like a slap in the face, I complained to God and to a friend who is a bishop: 'I'm finished. I just cannot go on like this.'

My friend listened: carefully, caringly. When my bitter saga ceased, he closed his eyes and I knew he was praying. A few minutes later, to my consternation and utter fury, he said: 'I believe you have simply to carry on as you are. Didn't Jesus say, "My meat is to do the will of him who sent me and to finish the work he gave me to do"? Your work is not finished yet. You must go back and serve others.'

For a couple of hours after that encounter, I remember tramping the hills of Derbyshire, railing at God, telling him it simply was not fair. But I went back, as instructed. Within minutes of my arrival home the 'phone rang. A person in considerable need was asking for help. When they came to see me, I thought I caught a glimpse of the reason why Jesus called obeying God 'meat'. In offering a supporting hand to this person, I found myself being fed, refreshed, renewed and supported by God. I began to learn that day that you cannot outgive God, neither can you waste love.

In the middle of writing this chapter, a similar thing happened. I have been plagued by loneliness, as I admitted earlier. Halfway through this chapter, the all-too-familiar waves began to sweep over me again. My neighbour, I knew, had just failed her driving test. She was miserable. 'It's terrible being a failure. It claws at your inside somehow.' I decided to pop in to see her. We sat in her kitchen drinking tea. She poured out the problems of her ghastly day: the test, the traffic jams, the dreaded news: 'Failed'. In listening to her woes, my loneliness disappeared. Another lesson was reinforced. Love is not dissipated when it is given away. It is replenished. If you want to find your way out of the maze of loneliness, therefore, you must give love. If you want a good friend, you must be one.

Enjoy the present
I am not pretending that this route out of loneliness is easy. I am claiming that it is well-tried and possible. In addition to taking the risk of faith, responding to the love of God, keep-

ing your feet on the rock-solid truth that you are not a cast-off, and reaching out to others, you can apply yourself continuously to that art I mentioned earlier: cultivating creative solitude.

One way to do this is to place a high value on the present: to refuse to live mainly in the future. Loneliness holds us in a vice-like grip when certain uncertainties pound through our brain relentlessly: 'Will God ever send a marriage partner?' 'In these days of high unemployment, will there *ever* be a niche for me?' 'How will I detect God's guidance when it does come?' We worry. We chafe. We sink into the slough of loneliness and the richness of 'the now' passes us by. Indeed 'the now' bears no more relevance to our lives than the countryside we zoom past on a journey in a super-fast Inter-city train.

This neglect of 'the now' presses on our existential loneliness and accentuates it. When we discover that the present moment is full of potential beauty, full of potential and profound pleasure, the pressure of loneliness is somehow relieved.

If you are reading this chapter because you, yourself, are searching for an exit from loneliness, try an experiment. Choose a favourite record or cassette. Play it, not as background music but as an unashamed activity: listening is an activity. Sit down. Concentrate fully on the music. Relish it. Enjoy it to the full.

Or choose one of your favourite pictures or posters. Really look at it: the colours, the texture, the hidden depths. Enjoy it. Or take a walk round your garden or a park, stop to smell the flowers. Touch them. Savour their delicate shades. Live each moment to the full like this, and loneliness creeps out of the back door while you are preoccupied with such satisfying pastimes.

Enjoy nature

I sometimes wonder whether this was what God was encouraging Job to do when he asked a string of questions: 'Has the rain a father? Who begets the dewdrops? What womb brings forth the ice, and gives birth to the frost of heaven, when the

waters grow hard as stone and the surface of the deep con-
geals? Can you fasten the harness of the Pleiades, or untie
Orion's bands?. . .Are you the one who makes the horse so
brave and covers his neck with flowing hair? Do you make
him leap like a grasshopper?' (Job 38:28–31; 39:19–20 JB).

I do not know what was in the mind of God. What I do
know is that the therapy worked. As God encouraged Job to
turn from his own inner confusion to contemplate nature, a
significant change took place. William Hulme puts it well:
'By turning his attention from his own misery to the marvels
of nature, Job's mind became open to the Spirit of God.
Through contemplating the fascinating variety within creation, he became reconciled to the Creator and received
peace.'[5]

Steeped in the world of nature, you find the courage to
open parts of yourself which must remain tightly closed in
the brashness of the city. Speaking personally, the therapy
which worked for Job works for me also. The countryside
where God's grandeur flames out[6] provides, not just peace,
but healing.

Pray the Psalms

I am not advocating a denial of our feelings of loneliness. We
may bump into them often. What I am suggesting is that we
recognize the inner pangs of loneliness, but rather than
capitulating to their demands, we press on. One way to do
this is to pray the Psalms. The psalmist experienced these
feelings we have described and is therefore capable of identifying with our hidden longings and sighs. But a psalm rarely
begins and ends with trouble. It often begins with expressed
sorrow, but by the time the psalmist has finished, it is relief,
even joy that he is experiencing.

Take Psalm 42, for example. The loneliness of the first
three verses gives way to hope. Before the psalm ends hope
has spawned confidence, even joy. Turn to this psalm when
loneliness clutches at your spirit. Or use Psalm 91 or Psalm
71 or Psalm 22 as a basis for your prayers.

As we take these positive steps from loneliness to the
creativeness of solitude we are not unlike children exploring

the Adventure Playground at Chatsworth House in Derby-shire. The course begins with a tunnel to crawl through. It continues with all manner of chutes and swings. You will often watch children, grim-faced and fearful, begin the initial tunnel crawl. Those same children will be full of smiles by the time they have completed the assignment.

The promise to us is somewhat similar. 'Your sorrow shall be turned to joy.' This joy is not dependent on emerging from the tunnel, though, as I have emphasized, we must work hard at doing that. No. The joy is dependent on being discovered by Jesus at every stage of the journey. And for those of us who are prone to loneliness, the Bible affords great comfort. It is full of examples of God, not ignoring man's loneliness, but touching him in the middle of it. I think of Elijah who, in the middle of his loneliness, was recommissioned by God. I think of Moses who, in the middle of his loneliness, heard the divine call. I think of Naomi who, in the middle of her loneliness, discovered that she was not forsaken by God, but chosen and blessed by him. And we think, supremely, of Jesus who sought solitude, who showed us that, if we are to be effective for God in the market place, we must find God in the secret space of our own hearts also.

While I have been writing this chapter, a hymn of Charles Wesley's has been running through my mind. You might like to use it when you feel lonely:

> Jesu, Lover of my soul,
>   Let me to thy bosom fly,
> While the nearer waters roll,
>   While the tempest still is high;
> Hide me, O my Saviour, hide,
>   Till the storm of life is past;
> Safe into the haven guide;
>   O receive my soul at last!
>
> Other refuge have I none;
>   Hangs my helpless soul on thee:
> Leave, ah! leave me not alone,
>   Still support and comfort me.

All my trust on thee is stay'd,
All my help from thee I bring:
Cover my defenceless head
With the shadow of thy wing!

Notes for chapter nine

1. All four quotations from Nicky Cruz, *Lonely but never Alone* (Pickering and Inglis, 1981), pp.69–72.
2. Elizabeth, quoted by David Atkinson in *The Message of Ruth: The Wings of Refuge* (IVP, 1983), pp.29–30.
3. Thomas à Kempis, *The Imitation of Christ* (Lakeland, 1979), pp.61–62.
4. For a fuller discussion of *how* to enter into this kind of stillness with God, see *Growing in Freedom* by Joyce Huggett (IVP, 1984).
5. William E. Hulme, *Creative Loneliness* (Lakeland, 1979), p.46.
6. Gerard Manley Hopkins' phrase.

10
An Offshoot of Loneliness: Masturbation

Loneliness drives people to find some kind of solace: it drives some to masturbate. In this chapter, we focus on that controversial, hush-hush subject, masturbation.

Among the pile of papers clamped together by the red bulldog clip I mentioned in the Preface lie some containing the following questions: 'I've heard a lot of gossip about masturbation. What exactly is it? Why do Christians do it? Is it wrong?' 'Some Christians say that masturbation is wrong, others say if I stop feeling guilty about it the problem will go away. I'm confused. What should I believe?' 'I feel so lonely without a partner, masturbation seems to be the only way I have of releasing tension. Is it sinful? I sometimes feel very guilty about it.'

These questions are typical of those I am asked regularly. I propose, therefore, to use this chapter to clarify what masturbation is and what it is not, to look at the question, 'Why do people masturbate?', to observe some effects of masturbatory activity and to seek to answer the vexed question, 'Is it a sin?'

What is masturbation?
This word 'masturbation' comes from two Latin words: *manus* meaning hand and *turbatio* meaning agitation or excitement. A person who masturbates is one who seeks sexual excitation through stimulating his or her own sex organs with his or her hands or fingers, or in some other way.

Many people object to the word 'masturbation' because, for centuries, it has carried negative overtones. They prefer to use one of a cluster of pseudonyms for this activity: self-stimulation, auto-stimulation, auto-eroticism, self-manipulation, solo-sexuality, to mention a few. These terms are used interchangeably to describe the genital activity I mentioned above.

It needs to be recognized, particularly in Christian circles where the very word 'masturbation' is taboo, that this practice of self-stimulation is perfectly normal in the sense that almost everybody does it at some stage in their life.

In his report, *Sexual behaviour in the human male*, A.C. Kinsey records the results of his research into masturbatory activity among college-level males. His findings suggest that 99% of such men are said to have nocturnal emissions, 96% practise masturbation and 80% of 'religiously active' men admitted to the practice of masturbation.[1] Another set of figures suggests that as many as 75% of women also masturbate.

Children masturbate. It is a part of their self-exploration. If they discover that playing with their genitals brings pleasure, it may become a natural part of pleasurable self-discovery for a while. There is nothing wrong with this child-play. It is not dirty. Children should not be scolded. They should be allowed to investigate their bodies in this way.

Adolescents masturbate for a different reason. They discover that self-stimulation can relieve them of a great deal of pent-up sexual tension. They, too, discover the pleasure involved. In the region of 90% of teenage boys masturbate for this reason. Like the self-discovery of childhood, this masturbatory activity during adolescence is part of the maturing process and should not be seen as cause for alarm or unnecessary guilt.

In adulthood, many people continue to masturbate. Many men masturbate to release the sperm which build up in the seminal vesicles every four or five days. Wet dreams, or nocturnal emissions to use the technical term, deal with some of this build-up, but even so some men find they need to resort to masturbation as an additional tension-reducer. They find that masturbation is more than a physiological necessity, but the needed release can come very quickly with minimal physical stimulation, non-erotic touch and in an emotional vacuum, that is, without erotic fantasies. Some women, too, masturbate regularly during certain stages of the menstrual cycle when sexual hunger is intense but when their needs cannot be met in any other way. Such solo-sex might take place in the 'quickie' way I described above, or it might become the climax of erotic fantasy.

Many married people masturbate. A man whose wife is in an advanced state of pregnancy and who might therefore find sexual intercourse uncomfortable might stimulate himself, or the couple might resort to mutual manual masturbation to orgasm, each bringing the other to a pleasurable climax manually rather than genitally. A husband who works away from home all week or who is away from home on business for a prolonged spell may masturbate, not simply to reduce tension but in order to keep alive his genital love for his wife. He may imagine his wife alongside him while he masturbates. His wife, similarly, may masturbate and wish that her husband were there with her. Or a widow may masturbate while fantasizing about her deceased partner. It may be one of the ways she copes with sexual frustration during the painful process of bereavement.

From childhood, through adolescence, into young adulthood, single people masturbate. Many married people phase in and out of masturbatory activity, too. And as we have seen, when their vocation changes from marriage back to singleness again, either because of separation, divorce or death, solo-sex seems an attractive option for those who once enjoyed genital intercourse.

This over-all view of solo-sex can increase our understanding of a much misunderstood part of life. It seems to point to the fact that masturbation is a bridge between the infantile need ingrained in all of us to explore the mystery of our bodies and the challenge of adulthood which confronts each of us to come to terms with our sexuality and see it as part of our personality. Solo-sex, then, should be seen as the bridge which links childhood and adulthood. Indeed, it should be seen as an exciting challenge: a challenge to grow towards maturity.

Thus the adolescent who masturbates must learn that,

pleasurable as the sensations of self-stimulation are, the chief purpose of the sex drive is not to gratify self but to move us towards others: not so that we use others' bodies for self-gratification either genitally or emotionally, but so that we learn, through joy and pain, what it means to give affection and receive it, so that we learn what it means to love as Jesus loves us.

We shall return to this process of integration later in this chapter. Here I simply want to make the point that masturbation or solo-sex is a common practice. Self-stimulation is not smutty or dirty, it is a part of most people's life at one time or another; the route many people take as they travel from immaturity and loneliness to personal integration and the wholeness God gives.

Having written all that I have, I also know many fine Christians who have never masturbated. That does not mean you are not normal. Nor does it mean you should experiment. Perhaps you could use this chapter to deepen your understanding of the masturbatory problem so that you are better equipped to help friends who may come to you plagued with guilt because, for them, masturbation seems a huge obstacle to overcome.

What masturbation is not

I have already said that masturbation is not dirty or despicable, like graffiti scribbled on toilet walls. Some people *feel* as though it is dirty. There are several possible reasons for this. One is that many Christians scarcely dare whisper the word 'masturbation' in Christian circles. Even in a counselling situation a person will come to me and say, 'My spiritual life is in a mess', rather than spell out the real problem: 'I'm plagued with guilt because of masturbation.' This hush-hush atmosphere is unhealthy and unhelpful and contributes to the fear that, if the word is taboo, it must point to a grievous sin. And for many of us, our background has added to the problem. When cleaning our genitals in infancy, our parents may have made their disgust known. We pick up the message: 'This part of me is foul.' We believe it. The message sticks. If our parents *see* us playing with our genitals, we might be slapped or told that we are naughty. Again, we register that for some reason this part of me is 'bad'. To compound the problem, few mature Christians ever admit that they have battled with masturbatory tendencies, so we draw the conclusion that we must be the only ones. We therefore paint a fearsome picture of ourselves: my private parts are foul yet I enjoy the sexual excitation they give me. No-one else shares this problem, and it is such a shameful sin that the church does not even mention it. I am through and through bad.

If this is the conclusion you have come to about yourself, it is perfectly understandable, but it is wrong. The truth is, as I have said, that solo-sex is common, a part of growing up, hushed up in the church because we have not yet learned to be real with each other, because we are afraid to call a spade a spade, because few people have taken the trouble to examine what masturbation is and what it is not. So let me underline the fact that masturbation is not the filthy, despicable practice some would suggest.

Not dangerous
Neither is it dangerous.

Perhaps another reason why the church is so slow to speak to the agony some people suffer over the masturbatory problem is that we have not yet recovered from the hangover of the past: the views about solo-sex held by the Victorians and their forbears.

Donald Goergen reminds us of the prejudiced and unscientific anti-masturbation propaganda popular in the late nineteenth century. He refers to a lecture given by Henry Varley in 1883 where the claim was made in public that epileptic fits, gonorrhoea and insanity were attributable to masturbation; that the loss of one drop of seminal fluid caused more bodily damage than the loss of forty drops of blood.

At the same period, the view was widely held that masturbation was a destructive sin; and that those who practised it were stooping to self-abuse. Old wives' tales convinced masturbators that blindness, barrenness and impotence were all caused by this deadly enemy.

Today we smile at these terror-inducing proscriptions. We recognize them for what they are: prejudiced nonsense. Today the pendulum has swung a long way away from this negativism. Young people are now being actively encouraged, by some, not simply to discount these *pro*scriptions but to view solo-sex as a health-giving *pre*scription. It is therapy, a journey into self-realization, a duty, some claim.

Not a panacea for all woes

In my view, the pendulum has swung too far. While we must refuse to listen to these old wives' tales or be bound by them, and while we must accept our genitalia as designed by God, fascinating, beautiful, we must also recognize the limitations and effects of self-stimulation. It is not the panacea for all woes some would claim. Unless we recognize this we shall not be motivated to move out of the solo-sex cul-de-sac on to the highway where we discover that sex is about loving others, not oneself.

One of the reasons why I resist the 'masturbation is healthy' voice is that, after adolescence, masturbation has little, if anything, to do with the fascination we feel for the mystery of growth, and instead it has much to do with expressing loneliness, a yearning for intimacy, anxiety and even depression. Indeed, for most adults, the kind of tension-relieving quickie solo-sex I described earlier is replaced by auto-eroticism of a rather different kind. Technically, the process is exactly the same: manual stimulation of the sex organs until a climax is enjoyed; but the context becomes the world of make-believe: fantasy. A man might masturbate while imagining himself having intercourse with a girl he fancies or with an imaginary person or with a pin-up or TV personality. A girl might masturbate while daydreaming about the boy she wishes to go out with, or a real or imaginary hero.

This kind of eroticism, like the more casual kind of auto-stimulation, is a language. The quickie variety could be saying nothing more profound than: 'My body is a mystery, fascinating. I'm glad to find an outlet for sexual steam.' The second, heavier kind, conveys a rather different message which must be interpreted accurately if we are to understand ourselves and others.

Martin Hallett, in his helpful paper 'Masturbation', makes this sensitive and accurate observation: 'Masturbation may be the presenting problem but it is not the real problem. The underlying problems are usually loneliness, lack of fulfilling relationships, lack of direction, interest and excitement in life. A lack of self-acceptance and feelings of inadequacy can also lead someone to resort to a fantasy world of sexual relationships. . . .'[2]

The chief problem with this fantasy world we create is that it has little to do with real life. Indeed, it makes the harsh reality of everyday life even more difficult to bear. In our fantasy world our partner desires us, expresses this desire flawlessly, brings perfect satisfaction. In this fantasy world there is a complete absence of pain and frustration. Thus, for a few precious moments our loneliness is alleviated by this imagined lover. The relationship we create is fulfilling. We find ourselves able to give love and receive it. Our secret world of make-believe offers colour, excitement, spice. Apart from the fact that it includes genital intercourse with a prohibited partner, which we shall look at later, this way of coping with life is as short-lived as the happiness a balloon gives to a child. A child adores a new balloon. But the shock and pain a child's face registers when the balloon pops is heart-breaking. And pricking the fantasy bubble is even more devastating. It does nothing to alleviate long-term loneliness: it adds to it. It does nothing to remove the sting of self-loathing: it accentuates it. Indeed it pushes some people deeper and deeper into the dark pit of introspection. That is why I put question marks over the 'masturbation is healthy' claim. Of itself masturbation is not unhealthy, but when accompanied by fantasy it is not healthy either. But is it a sin? Christians need an answer to this question: Is masturbation a sin?

Is masturbation sinful?

The church, as ever, is divided over this question. In certain circles the following dogma is still taught:

Masturbation is objectively a serious sin. Except in rare cases, it is also subjectively sinful, and the average person who gives in to masturbation, either as a teenager or as an adult, commits sin.[3]

Many Christian leaders today challenge this blanket condemnation. John White, for example, says in *Eros Defiled:* 'Masturbation is not, in and of itself, sin at all. Yet many people are convinced that it is sin and feel guilty when they masturbate.'[4] And William Kraft goes further when he observes:

In the recent past, masturbation was often considered one of the worst sins. When people masturbated, they neither passed go nor collected 200 dollars, but went straight to hell and often died of guilt on the way. Many contemporary approaches go almost to the opposite extreme by considering masturbation as a sensible source of pleasure, a convenient tension-reducer or a way to realize body potential. Many mental health specialists say that it is a healthy practice.[5]

Some say solo-sex is sin. Some say solo-sex is not a sin. Some say solo-sex is healthy.

What does the Bible say?

Before agreeing or disagreeing with such conclusions, we need to examine what the Bible says about the practice of masturbation. Most Christians, particularly those who have been burdened with guilt on account of masturbatory activity, find it hard to believe that the word masturbation is not even mentioned by the Bible writers. If you search for clear guidelines there, you will draw a blank. The 'Thou shalt not masturbate' verse does not exist. The claim that masturbation is a sin of the most grievous nature cannot, therefore, be substantiated by Scripture. Indeed, the view that to masturbate is to commit sin is not biblical either.

What the Bible does make crystal clear is that the kind of fantasies I described earlier are forbidden. In Matthew

5:27–28, for example, Jesus says: ' "You have heard that it was said, 'Do not commit adultery.' But now I tell you: anyone who looks at a woman and wants to possess her is guilty of committing adultery with her in his heart" ' (GNB).

As we have already seen, when we masturbate in our cosy fantasy world, we do possess the prohibited partner and are possessed by them. In Jesus' view, such imaginations fall into the category of committing adultery in the heart. In Jesus' view, such adulterous thoughts should be purged. 'So if your right eye causes you to sin, take it out and throw it away! It is much better for you to lose a part of your body than to have your whole body thrown into hell' (Matthew 5:29 GNB). This strong language does not mean that we literally gouge out our wayward eyes or castrate ourselves. It does mean that we deal with the fantasies and refuse to be held captive by them.

But what of the physical act itself : self-manipulation as a physiological necessity? Is this wrong? Or isn't it?

The Bible leaves us in no doubt about what sin is: that which corrupts and spoils the life of each person born into the world; rebellion against God. The Bible does not hesitate to label specific sins: neglect of parents, abandonment of widows, refusal to obey those in authority, greed, discontentment, lying, promiscuity, adultery, unkindness, bitterness, hatred, resentment, obscene language and so on. The list is long. But the list nowhere includes a hint of tension-relieving masturbation.

Indeed, the question needs to be asked whether the act, of itself, is not unlike scratching your head to relieve an itch, sneezing or stretching after a period of prolonged inactivity.

Whether these are accurate parallels or not, it seems safe to assume that, since God is not in the habit of leaving us in doubt about the nature of sin, the practice of releasing pent-up genital tension is not, of itself, a sin. It does not fall into the 'defilement' category described by Jesus in Mark 7:21-23: ' "It is what comes out of a person that makes him unclean" ' (verse 20 GNB). It should not, therefore, provide an occasion for guilt.

Dr Leslie Weatherhead once summed up the situation well. When someone put the question to him: 'Is masturbation a sin or not?', he replied: 'It depends whether the picture on the screen of the mind at the time could be shown to our Lord without shame.' If there is no picture on the wall, refuse to be weighed down by guilt. Too many Christians known to me wallow in unnecessary guilt about masturbation and forget that God may be wanting them to deal with other problems in their lives. But of course if the picture on the wall is of someone else's partner or a person to whom you are not married, whether that person is imaginary or real, then a way out of the problem must be found.

We shall explore some possible exits later in this chapter. First, I want to pin-point several other reasons why it may be necessary to search for ways of abandoning masturbatory activity.

The first is that masturbation can become an obsession. It can become compulsive, even addictive. As such, it becomes a kind of bondage which holds us in its grip. No Christian should be content to remain in bondage to any habit or way of life which denies them the joy of the freedom Jesus bought for them on Calvary.

Another reason why some Christians may want to turn their back on self-stimulation is that, at best, it is love turned in on itself, and at worst, it is narcissism, inappropriate love of self. As Christians, our goal in life is to become more like Jesus. In the wilderness temptation Jesus set us a fine example of what it means to struggle against self-gratification; to refuse to live for self-gratification alone.

A third reason why masturbation may need to be shed as an outgrown pastime is that, when fantasy is involved, it becomes a form of idolatry in which the imaginary people become sex idols and sex objects. This, of itself, debases our view of people created by God and turns people into playthings. But worse, it prompts us, if an opportunity arises, to translate our fantasy into activity, thus overemphasizing the romantic and the genital in what could be a healthy, supportive friendship.

Some ways out of masturbation

'But how do you kick the habit? I've tried everything I know but nothing seems to work. I gain the victory for a few days, then I find myself slipping back into old patterns of behaviour.'

Such confessions are not rare. I do not believe they are lame excuses. When masturbation has become a habit, it is difficult to uproot: difficult, but not impossible.

First, we shall consider some possible practical ways out of masturbatory activity. Martin Hallett, in his paper entitled 'Masturbation', suggests that the person seeking to break free from the masturbatory pattern of behaviour should first seek to break the association of ideas. If bedtime spells masturbation, introduce another activity into the bedtime routine.

I think of a friend of mine who wrote to me late one night and admitted that this letter-writing routine was an attempt to break this association of ideas; to cut himself free from the masturbatory activity which seemed to have a firm hold on him.

Margaret Evening, in her book *Who Walk Alone*, also suggests that activities like reading a book (though not a romantic one), planning shopping lists, balancing the budget, designing a dress, might help to engage the mind until a stage of exhaustion is reached which guarantees sleep and eliminates the need to masturbate. For those who are unable to keep the light on late, she suggests a series of mental gymnastics in the dark!

Go back in memory to some moment of *pure* joy and relive that experience: a legitimate use of the gift of memory. Go back to holiday experiences – a mountain walk in clean, fresh air, a swim in warm, blue sea, a promenade concert, or an exciting discovery. Use every imaginative power to conjure up the sights, sounds, smells, feel of fresh air, the taste of different food, the wind in the hair, the lovely burning of a sun tan. These are bodily delights in which there is no shame. If your imagination is going to get to work anyway, make it work the way *you* choose and keep hard at it so that thoughts don't slip off onto unscheduled paths.[7]

If these practical suggestions help, then use them. But recognize, too, that if you masturbate regularly and if this genital activity takes place in the context of erotic fantasy, to deal with the overt genital activity is to tackle only the surface problem. It is essential not just to pluck off the part of the weed which you see, but to deal with the taproot. This is far from easy.

Use of fantasy

One powerful way to counteract the problem is to use fantasy to combat fantasy. Let me explain what I mean by this.

You have been living in a dream world where the perfect lover satisfies your emotional and genital needs. You can do three things with this realization. Repress it, confess it, or listen to its hidden message.

It is useless to repress such behaviour: to pretend this activity is not a part of your life. Confess it to yourself and to God. Don't wallow in self-pity or self-recrimination. Rather, recognize that failure of this kind is almost always a language, and determine to listen to the many layers of communication hidden here.

If you listen carefully, you will almost certainly hear the inner you admitting the yearning for intimacy with a person of the opposite sex, admitting the readiness to receive and give such intimacy, admitting that the absence of this much desired 'other' creates loneliness.

Instead of regressing into a fantasy world where these needs can be met, though all too inadequately as we have seen, determine to act upon the message which your sexual desire has articulated. Re-read chapter nine of this book. Discover how your loneliness can be met with fulfilling friendships, healing activities and encounters and resolve to reach out to others, not for genital intimacy, but for the emotional, spiritual and aesthetic intimacy we looked at in the earlier chapters of this book. Do not look on the masturbatory problem as an enemy. Rather, see it as the faithful friend who ever presses us to widen our horizons, who ever encourages us to discover our full potential, who ever persuades us to grow in maturity and in the likeness of Christ.

When you are tempted to fantasize or begin to feel unhelpful thoughts crowd into your mind, there is value in forcing yourself to sit up in bed, maybe even to switch on the light. Ask yourself: Who is playing the leading role in my dream world this time? Why is it this particular person? Why am I resorting to this kind of eroticism? What is so special about my dream world? What, in comparison, makes the real world so drab and unattractive? What can I do to brighten my real world?

Such a procedure is drastic. You may have to force yourself to do it, but it is far more wholesome than resorting to secret love affairs of which you will be ashamed before God on waking next morning.

Listen to the language of guilt

If fantasy contains a message, so does guilt. Almost all Christians who masturbate feel guilty. The most efficient method of dealing with guilt is to listen to its accusing voice and to try to assess, from an objective point of view, whether these accusations are accurate or not. This is vital. Unless you do this, guilt about masturbation will exert the emotional pressure which will, in turn, create the tension which pushes you into masturbation. This vicious circle must be interrupted, not perpetuated.

Perhaps guilt has been persuading you that you are dirty, for reasons I explained earlier in this chapter? Reject such accusations. Do not collude with them by admitting your culpability. Perhaps your parents were the kind who, even when you became an adult, always switched off the radio if sex was mentioned, or changed channels if erotic scenes appeared on television? Perhaps you gained the impression from this embarrassed behaviour that genitalia are shameful, that *your* sexuality is an embarrassment? Again, reject such attitudes. This is prudery and Victorianism, not the acceptance of our sexuality which is essential to emotional health and wholeness.

But maybe guilt reminds you of your obsession with self, or of the fact that your fantasy world is a tawdry substitute for the real thing. If guilt points out such failure, don't wallow. Admit your culpability and, as you confess, ask God to show you how to take the kind of risks with friendship we have observed in earlier chapters of this book. Be excited that you are on the threshold of new discoveries in this field.

Keep clear of things which arouse

If you are serious about discovering an exit from the masturbatory maze, determine to steer clear of situations which you know will make temptation difficult to resist. I think of one young man who resolved, this time, to gain the victory. 'We'll have to stop wandering in and out of each other's bedrooms,' he said to his girlfriend. 'Seeing you in your nightshirt finishes me.'

It is one thing to make these resolves, quite another to put them into practice. But such discipline is essential. Indeed, discipline is the key to success.

Discipline can be fun. Discipline is not the same as repressing hostile emotions. Discipline acknowledges sexual urges, accepts them, affirms them, then chooses, quite deliberately, to deny them the pleasure of expression. In other words, discipline is lying in bed, listening to the inner clamour, the desire to masturbate, acknowledging that those feelings belong to you, but rising above them and telling them gently but firmly, 'I know perfectly well what you want but I am not capitulating to your demands today.' Such discipline is healthy, liberating, fulfilling. It assures you that you are not controlled by your genital urges but that you are in control. Such discipline, as William Kraft describes it, is simply putting your sexuality in brackets. Such discipline is the basis of all freedom.

Rechannel the energy

When we grow more experienced in the art of disciplining our sexual urges we also become more skilled at rechannelling all this energy into other activities. Such rechannelling should not be a result of pretence: 'Let's pretend we are not sexually aroused today.' No. Such sublimation, as it is called, recognizes the full force of the genital desire but recognizes also that it would be inappropriate to give those desires expression and therefore seeks other avenues: social, cultural, physical, aesthetic, spiritual, into which to channel surplus energy.

Mortify the flesh

Another way to deal with this particular habit is to put it to death, to mortify it. Paul makes it clear that in certain areas of our lives, to deal such death-blows is vital. 'If you live according to your human nature, you are going to die; but if by the Spirit you put to death your sinful actions, you will live' (Romans 8:13 GNB). 'You must put to death, then, the earthly desires at work in you, such as sexual immorality, indecency, lust, evil passions. . .' (Colossians 3:5 GNB).

When Paul exhorts us to put such activity to death, he is not advocating playing games: 'I have no more need for genital gratification'. What it involves is recognizing to the full the urgent need you have, from time to time, to give your genital desires full expression, but at the same time refusing to give such urges space in your life and refusing to feed them so that they weaken and wither until an appropriate time for their full expression presents itself.

Prune your activity

Another way out of the masturbation problem is to resolve to cut down on your masturbatory activity but in doing so, to prune first those activities which are combined with fantasy rather than those which simply relieve tension.

It also helps to share the problem with one or two trusted friends, to ask them to pray for you, to ask them to help you to keep your eyes firmly fixed on Jesus while you seek to integrate your sexuality and your spirituality. I know it will not be easy to break the sound barrier and mention the dreaded word 'masturbation', but I firmly believe that if you pluck up courage and mention your struggles in this area others would identify with your frustration, pray for you and support you.

Some facts to remember

Many, many fellow pilgrims are stumbling along the route to maturity. Most discover that progress in this particular area of spiritual maturity is often slow. Instead of giving in to discouragement, therefore, remember that very often God gives, not immediate victory, but the courage and ability to try again after a period of failure.

Whenever you fail, Satan, the great Accuser, will not be far away, whispering lies and condemnation. 'You're a hypocrite. You'll never make it.' Instead of caving in, resist the devil and he will slink away. Recall the fact of the matter: you do not have to remain in bondage to the practice of masturbation. Bit by bit, you can replace fantasy relationships with real, affectionate friendships. Meanwhile your body will not burst from sexual tension even though it might feel as though it might from time to time.

I sometimes fear for young Christians determined to deal the death-blow to masturbation. Their personal crusade is engaged on such an intense level that I sometimes question whether they are even conscious of other far more deadly beams jutting out of their eyes. It is worth asking, 'Is masturbation the biggest blockage in my life, Lord, or is there something else which needs urgent attention first?' We must remember that God is far less harsh with us than some of us are with ourselves. He wants us to enjoy the freedom he won for us.

In our spiritual journey we are not unlike the tadpoles I was watching just before I began to write this chapter. Some were small and skinny, others were big and plump. Some seemed almost ready to sprout their first leg. Some would soon be completely transformed into frogs. No-one chastised the tiny tadpoles for lagging behind their bigger brothers. Each had reached a fascinating stage of growth. And so have we. We must therefore hold two things in tension: the patience to wait God's timing for our spiritual spurt of growth, and the discontentment which ensures that we do everything in our power to ensure that this growth will happen. And whenever we fail, some words from a Marilyn Baker song can encourage us to begin again:

When you feel that you just can't pray,
You've grieved the Lord and he seems so far away,

Don't lose hope, for he wants to say,
'My child just begin again.'
When you feel you can't try anymore,
It seems you've failed so many times before,
God still loves you, he's the door
For you to begin again.

(From *Whispers of God*)

Notes for chapter ten

1. A.C. Kinsey, *Sexual Behaviour in the Human Male* (1948), p.503.
2. Martin Hallett, 'Masturbation' (available from True Freedom Trust).
3. Quoted by Donald Goergen in *The Sexual Celibate* (Seabury Press, 1974), pp.199–200.
4. John White, *Eros Defiled* (IVP, 1978), p.38.
5. William F. Kraft, *Sexual Dimensions of the Celibate Life* (Gill & Macmillan, 1979), p.145.
6. Quoted by Margaret Evening in *Who Walk Alone* (Hodder and Stoughton, 1974), p.32.
7. *Who Walk Alone*, p.34.

11
Another Offshoot of Loneliness: Homosexuality

Loneliness creates in some a hunger for genital involvement with a person of the opposite sex. Loneliness creates in others a yearning for genital involvement with a person of the same sex.

In this chapter, I plan to direct the spotlight on to that much misunderstood and feared word, 'homosexuality'. We shall examine certain questions which are frequently raised today: 'What exactly is homosexuality?' 'What does the Bible say about homosexuals?' 'Is homosexuality a sin?' 'How can the Christian fellowship best help those with a homosexual orientation?' 'How should a person with a homosexual bias view himself?' 'Are there escape routes from homosexuality?' 'What is the purpose of same-sex friendships?' 'How does one deal with the fear of homosexuality?' Not everyone will agree with my answers to these questions. You must decide for yourself whether what I suggest seems biblical and sensible. What follows is the fruit of much thinking about this subject: reflections which have arisen from counselling people troubled by this expression of loneliness.

What is homosexuality?
Mention the word 'homosexuality' in any mixed gathering of people and you can almost guarantee reactions as mixed as the persons present: revulsion, horror, acceptance, understanding, bewilderment, prejudice, mirth and possibly a defence of homosexual activity may be expressed. The words perversion, evil, disease, sin, may all be used to describe the

homosexual condition. Some may even describe homosexuality as 'normal'; particularly those who are practising homosexuals: those who feel guilty or trapped by their own behaviour.

But what *is* the homosexual condition? Again, definitions vary. *The Gay Manifesto* describes homosexuality as 'the capacity to love someone of the same sex'.[1] Against this broadest of backcloth definitions, John White narrows homosexuality down to genital activity: 'A homosexual act is one designed to produce sexual orgasm between members of the same sex. A homosexual is a man or woman who engages in homosexual acts.'[2] William Kraft seems to agree with this narrow definition. He claims that 'strictly speaking, homosexuality means homogenitality. Those who choose a homosexual life-style indicate that sexually they prefer and desire genital relations with a member of the same sex. With the latter homosexuals feel comfortable and affirmed, while with the opposite sex they feel uncomfortable, impotent, resentful, scared or simply indifferent when genital relations are possible. When people consistently, and over a long period of time, yearn to be genitally intimate and behave genitally with the same sex, they are true homosexuals. . . .The life-styles of homosexuals are permeated with and motivated by genital relations with the same sex, rather than being periodic. Especially when lonely, empty or depressed, homosexuals turn to a sexual relationship with a member of the same sex as their saving grace.'[3]

While this definition is accurate enough, it must also be recognized that some people with a homosexual orientation also enjoy sexual relations with persons of the opposite sex.

The definitions fan out into a broader pattern again with Donald Goergen's own definition: the homosexual is 'one whose primary emotion and erotic interest is directed towards a member of the same sex'[4], and with Elizabeth Moberly's claim that 'homosexuality is not essentially a sexual condition'.[5] Elizabeth Moberly's thesis is that a true homosexual is a person who has suffered the loss or the absence of same-sex parental love during the formative years; a person, therefore, who remains in a state of incompleteness and who searches for completion in relationships with persons of the same sex in adulthood. In her important book, based on eight years of research into the homosexual condition, she uses such phrases as 'a hurtful experience', 'intrapsychic damage at a deep level', 'hidden orphans', those with 'a need for love' to describe persons with a homosexual orientation. Elizabeth Moberly, a Christian research psychologist in Cambridge specializing in psychoanalytic developmental psychology, concludes that homosexuality is not caused by genetic imbalance nor by hormone imbalance, nor through abnormal learning processes, but almost always by lack of love from someone of the same sex.

By making this claim, Elizabeth Moberly is not encouraging people with a homosexual bias to blame their parents for lack of warmth or care. Neither is she encouraging parents of adults burdened by a homosexual problem to become guilt-ridden by the apparent failure of the past. What she is implying is that this deficit of same-sex parent love is often subtle; the deficit might have been the paucity of the love offered or it might have been the child's perception which was at fault – his inability to respond to the style of parental loving being offered. It often happens, therefore, that when the 'hidden orphan' living within the adult begins to understand why their parents acted in the way they did, and when they are prepared to forgive their parents for the hurt inflicted, healing becomes a very real possibility.

Is homosexuality a sin?
Before we decide whether homosexuality is, of itself, a sin, definitions must be carefully considered.

If you take the broad view painted by *The Gay Manifesto*, clearly homosexual feelings are not abnormal. As Henri Nouwen rightly points out, such same-sex loving is common to all healthy, growing persons:

> When we are still struggling with finding out who we really are, homosexual feelings can be just as strong as heterosexual feelings. There is nothing abnormal about

homosexual feelings at a time in which our life has not yet formed a definite pattern. Perhaps the absence of these feelings is more abnormal than their presence.[6]

And, as we shall go on to observe later in this chapter, same-sex friendships contribute a valuable ingredient of love to our lives at various stages of the maturing process.

Warm feelings for members of the same sex are not sinful. If they were, the Bible would not have described the friendship between David and Jonathan in such graphic detail and in such warm, approving language. 'Jonathan became one in spirit with David, and he loved him as himself. . . .And Jonathan made a covenant with David because he loved him as himself' (1 Samuel 18:1,3; see also 1 Samuel 20:4–42; 2 Samuel 1:23–27). Neither would the close friendship between John and Jesus or Lazarus and Jesus or Peter and Jesus have been unveiled.

Clearly these relationships were not sinful. They were emotionally intimate. The Bible is never anti-friendship. The Bible does not even condemn the homosexual orientation which some adults clearly have. What the Bible does rule out of court is homosexual genital activity.

What does the Bible teach?

There are seven references to homosexuality in the Bible: Genesis 19:1–11; Leviticus 18:22 and 20:13; Judges 19: 22–25; Romans 1:26–27; 1 Corinthians 6:9; 1 Timothy 1:9–11. To quote from just one: 'Do you not know that the wicked will not inherit the kingdom of God? Do not be deceived: Neither the sexually immoral nor idolaters nor adulterers nor male prostitutes nor homosexual offenders nor thieves nor the greedy nor drunkards nor slanderers nor swindlers will inherit the kingdom of God' (1 Corinthians 6:9–10). This strong, prohibitive language is typical of the Bible's attitude to homosexual genital activity. But it is not the homosexual condition which is condemned. What is judged is the genital activity which has been snatched from the context God meant it for: marriage. What is also condemned is the anti-God rebellion which so often accompanies homosexual genitality. Paul describes the situation well: 'They exchanged the truth of God for a lie, and worshipped and served created things rather than the Creator. . . .Because of this, God gave them over to shameful lusts. . . .Men committed indecent acts with other men, and received in themselves the due penalty for their perversion' (Romans 1:25–27).

What makes homosexuality sinful is precisely the same thing as makes heterosexuality sinful: not the condition, not the genital desire, not the attraction, but the inappropriate expression of the genital desire, the physical contact which demonstrates a lack of respect of the partner by using his body as a toy and by expressing affection in a way which is permissible only in the marriage relationship.

What does the Bible imply?

In the present debate in society about homosexuality, the claim is often made that a homosexual was created by God with that particular orientation and he should be encouraged, therefore, to accept his sexual orientation and to live within its limits.

The Bible does not seem to support this claim. Nowhere is the impression given that God made certain men and women with a homosexual orientation. On the contrary, in Genesis 1 we find God creating male and female in his own image and in Genesis 2 the male and female were attracted to one another like two magnets. Elizabeth Moberly concludes from this, and I agree with her, 'God did not create homosexuals *as* homosexuals, but as men and women who are intended to attain psychological maturity in their gender identity.' In other words, to claim that the person with a homosexual condition was created that way is to lack compassion and to deny the person the opportunity to respond to the challenge of the homosexual condition: to seek the touches from God which will enable that person to grow emotionally and spiritually and which will eventually result in greater wholeness and freedom.

Moreover, if we take Elizabeth Moberly's compassionate and persuasive definition of homosexuality as a working definition, that is, a homosexual person is one who has suffered a lack of same-sex parental loving in the formative years and who, though an adult, still tries to compensate for this childhood lack, then the Bible has a great deal to say to the homosexual and the homosexual condition.

If we can move in our thinking beyond the homogenital act to the homosexual person, and if we contemplate that person's inner need, seeing him as 'the hidden orphan', it becomes clear that the Bible's attitude to such persons is one of protective, unconditional love. This love stems from God's love. 'He defends the cause of the fatherless. . .' (Deuteronomy 10:18 and Psalm 10:18); 'The Lord. . .sustains the fatherless. . .' (Psalm 146:9). God himself is 'A father to the fatherless' (Psalm 68:5); in God 'the fatherless find compassion' (Hosea 14:3). Or, as some translators reword that verse, 'In thee the fatherless find a father's love.'

In the Bible's view, those who have been denied the warmth of adequate parental loving in childhood are to be offered love, not by God only, but by brothers and sisters in Christ also. The Bible exhorts us to 'encourage the oppressed', to 'defend. . .the fatherless' (Isaiah 1:17), to 'look after orphans. . .in their distress' (James 1:27).

Clearly, God does not want the emotional growth of a person to be stunted by a lack of love, whether this is through the physical loss of parents, through death (the normal interpretation given to this word orphan), or through the deficit caused through parental neglect, maltreatment, or a child's misinterpretation of parental love.

Whether a person's parents were guilty of wilful neglect or not matters little. What makes a person a 'hidden orphan' is not wilful negligence but the inability of the parent of the same sex to communicate the vital message, 'I love you'; or the inability of the child to absorb that life-giving message. For unless we *felt* loved by the parent of the same sex at the stage in our growth when it really mattered, that is, in the formative years, whether we were loved or not is immaterial. We need to *feel* loved in order to be assured that we *are* loved.

The key figures in our lives, therefore, need to learn to communicate the 'I love you' message in a way we can understand and accept. In the absence of this loving ingredient, something within us withers.

The responsibility of the Christian fellowship

We have seen that the homosexual condition is not unlike fatherlessness or motherlessness. We have also seen that we have a responsibility to persons suffering from such inner pain: to help them, to love them, to heal their wounds. This is the primary role of the church and fellowship groups when faced with a person admitting to a homosexual orientation.

The tragedy is that the church has not yet caught a vision of this God-given role. Instead, Christians mutter and quarrel about the surface problem: the genital expression which frequently accompanies the emotional deprivation. In attempting to stamp out the genital activity, in focusing their attention on one manifestation of the homosexual problem, they have made as their main mission the attempt to expose homogenital activity for what it is: sin, but at the same time have caused persons with a homosexual condition, hurting, smarting, love-hungry people, to form ghettos where they can be assured of some sort of understanding and care. As more than one homosexual has expressed it, 'I went out looking for a partner because I needed to feel the warmth of human arms around me.'

The urgent need in the church today, as I see it, is for a radical review of our attitude to Christians struggling with a homosexual problem.

What is needed, first and foremost, is a clear, informed, compassionate understanding of the nature and complexity of the homosexual condition. We need to see beyond the oral sex and the anal sex and the cottaging and the prostitution which are by-products of a deep-seated problem. We need to refuse ourselves permission to recoil from a brother or sister in Christ who confesses to homosexual tendencies. We need to see homosexuality for what it is: a challenge to grow, just as certain irregularities in heterosexual loving are challenges to grow.

There is little point in recognizing that a certain problem offers the opportunity for a spurt in growth unless we are prepared to offer the vital ingredients which precipitate that growth. Speaking personally, I long for the day when, in Christian fellowship groups, a person with a homosexual orientation, or a person plagued with a masturbatory problem, will be able to share this with the entire group and be certain that the confession will be met, not with condemnation, disapproval or a judgmental attitude, but with the assurance of help, and the prayer which heals: 'We're on your side. Thank you for being so open. We'll pray you through to the next stage of maturity.'

When such groups begin to function well, they will provide friendships for the homosexual person. This is what he needs and needs desperately. (I use the term 'he' here, but of course, not all homosexuals are male. The lesbian is a woman who gravitates towards another woman for emotional and sexual intimacy.) Indeed, the first phase of healing may well come, not through prayer, but through wholesome, non-genital relationships with people of the same sex.

The same-sex element is vital. We sometimes make the mistake of thinking, 'What he really needs is a girlfriend'; 'What the lesbian needs is a boyfriend'. There is a grain of truth in those beliefs but there is a 'not yet' element in the beliefs also. What a person with homosexual tendencies needs most is a loyal, understanding friend who will begin to meet his legitimate needs for same-sex loving which have not yet been adequately met. If this lack of love can be met in a non-genital way, these friendships will promote the emotional growth of the homosexual person.

Unshockability

When we learn to understand some of the complexities of the homosexual problem and when we grow to love individuals with a homosexual orientation, we give to them a valuable gift: the freedom to talk. We must become unshockable.

Many homosexuals bottle everything up inside them: their desire for genitality, their shame and self-loathing, their dread, and the fear that they will never marry or have children of their own. Through listening, we can unlock these prisons of loneliness and give love and understanding, support and care, friendship and ongoing prayer. The homosexual may never have experienced this quality of love. He may often have felt like a fringe person, an observer, always on the sidelines looking in. This free-flowing friendship, of itself, will engender hope, and the courage to try to change. Just as the heterosexual person needs another person and a place where they can voice the inner struggles which accompany the genital urges and the emotional temptations attached to sexual awakening, so the person with aroused homosexual desire must find a forum where he can tell it like it is and be heard.

The need for friendship

My fear is that unless we, in the church, offer such support to persons passing through the homosexual developmental phase of growth, the homosexual problem amongst Christians will grow.

Since the Wolfenden Report in 1954, the public acceptance of homosexuality in Britain has increased. Gay clubs, gay bars, gay marriages are all the rage. The gay lifestyle is positively promoted in the big cities of our land. Because gays have 'come out' it is now fashionable to talk about homosexuality. The symptoms of the homosexual condition are published, available for all to see.

The problem here is that, just as if you read a medical manual you can convince yourself that you are suffering from cancer or ulcers or glandular fever or other medical diseases, so the young person who is bridging the gap between childhood and full-grown adulthood can easily be beguiled into believing they are homosexual when they are not.

Homosexuality is a phase we all go through. The schoolgirl enjoys a series of 'crushes' or 'pashes' on older girls or teachers at school; boys might indulge in genital activity in the toilets, changing rooms or woods. This does not mean that they are confirmed homosexuals. It does mean that they are in transit, on the way to further sexual discoveries: the God-given joys of heterosexuality.

One set of figures produced by Kinsey when he researched

into the genital activity of men and women, suggested that 37% of males had indulged in genital activity with other men at some stage of their life. This did not fix them into a homosexual pattern. Most moved on to marriage and parenthood. That is why I say that homosexuality of this nature is sexual awareness *in transit*; it is one part of the tunnel which connects childhood and the heterosexual experience of adulthood, or the fulfilment of creative singleness and celibacy.

We shall look at ways of combating this fear of homosexuality later. Here I simply want to underline what I said earlier, that our responsibility as Christians is to understand the depth of the homosexual problem, to do everything in our power to meet the emotional needs of the person with a homosexual orientation, to provide an atmosphere where such persons can unburden themselves, and to further such persons' growth so that they, like us, learn to integrate sexuality and spirituality, sexuality and personality; so that homosexuality becomes a crisis of growth, not a crisis of decay.

The value of friendship

These same-sex friendships are of inestimable value to the person with a homosexual orientation for a number of reasons: for the sustenance offered in the present, for the security they afford for the future, and for the provision of love not received in the past.

One of my burdens as I write this book is to communicate and underline the sober fact that 'it is not good for man to be alone'; to emphasize that God did not equip us to go it alone. The tragedy is that, in certain circles, the Christian homosexual is forced to live a Jekyll and Hyde existence, forced to pretend to be one thing in public while hiding his true sex identity and behaving quite differently in secret. When the gulf between what he is and what he pretends to be grows bigger and bigger and bigger, the level of inner loneliness rises. The dread: 'If they really knew what I was like they wouldn't want me', takes root.

One of the purposes of true friendship is that we can share our secret sins, our feelings of failure, our hidden heartaches with our friend and know that this person will not reject us. Everyone needs such a friend. The homosexual is no exception. On the contrary, he probably needs such a friend more than most.

Facing the future

With such a friend or friends, we can face the future. We know that their love will cushion us from some of the knocks of life. We know that if we go away, they will still be there on our return, loving, caring, keeping our best interests in their hearts and prayers. People who have such friends are rich. They know that someone in this world outside the commitment of marriage is prepared to sacrifice for them, sympathize and empathize with them, and steady them during times of uncertainty.

And these friendships, of themselves, begin to heal over some of the wounds of the past. This is vital. What happens very often with the homosexual person is that, in the absence of same-sex parental love at a crucial stage in his emotional development, he deliberately unhitches himself from that parent figure to avoid being further hurt. Elizabeth Moberly calls this 'defensive detachment'. Instead of looking, in future, for love and support from the parent of the same sex, the child will attach himself to the parent of the opposite sex and rely on her for all his hunger for love to be satisfied. This detachment and attachment leaves an inner emptiness. At the adolescent stage of growth, when the glandular urges indicate that a sexual springtime has arrived, the homosexual does not search for the intimacy we described in chapter one, with a person of the *opposite* sex. (He has a partner of the opposite sex in this all-sufficient parent figure.) No. He yearns for that which he has never yet experienced: same-sex love. Because the accent, in the teenage and young adult years, is on genitalia and the genital expression of love, if the opportunity arises he will translate this deep desire into homosexual genitality.

What non-erotic same-sex friendships provide is the love he never experienced in the formative years. This sort of love, if care is taken not to permit such friendships to become genital, and if they avoid the danger of becoming imitations of immature puppy-love, can encourage the homosexual to detach himself, in a healthy and necessary way, from the parent figure of the opposite sex and to attach himself in a healthy way to members of his own sex. But this all takes time. The route is fraught with dangers. Where it works, it prepares the person with the problem to seek more permanent ways out of the homosexual orientation.

Some suggested escape routes

The good news for people with a homosexual orientation is that healing is available for those who want to avail themselves of it. The bad news is that it often takes a very long time, years rather than months, for a person to slide along the sexual scale. The good news is that everyone can move from one notch on the scale to another. The bad news is that practising homosexuals may have considerable difficulty, at first, abstaining from genital activity which seems to bring them sexual excitement, even fulfilment.

When we speak of healing, we are not speaking of healing the homosexual condition; it is not a disease, like cancer, so it cannot therefore be healed. What we are describing is the process by which the root causes of homosexuality can be touched. At the root, very often, as we have seen, lie wounds that will not stop bleeding. This is where the healing balm needs to be applied.

And when I speak of the sexual sliding scale, I have in mind Kinsey's suggestion that every person sits, most of the time, on a certain point of the slide-rule. But this sexual orientation is not fixed. A married person, to all intents and purposes happily heterosexual, might suddenly find herself physically attracted to another woman, even tempted to give that affection genital expression. She would move along the sliding scale several spaces but would probably revert after a period of time to her former heterosexual level. In the same way, a person with a homosexual orientation can be nudged along the slide-rule to a new fixed point. But, as I suggested, it takes time, patience and the healing hand of God.

John White and Elizabeth Moberly admit that, so far,

secular therapies like psychoanalysis have proved comparatively ineffective in the healing process. One of the reasons for this is that the aim of the treatment therapies is to bring about a quick sexual reorientation in the person concerned; to bring them from homosexuality to heterosexuality in a short space of time. As Elizabeth Moberly points out, this leaves the root problem, the lack of love from a person of the same sex, untouched. Marriage to a partner of the opposite sex does little to meet the legitimate needs for growth which have never been satisfied.

Meet the deficit

As we have already observed, the urgent need, therefore, is to meet the deficit of love; to provide the homosexual person with a friend, or preferably a group of friends, of the same sex who will meet him at various points of need.

The value of such friendships was highlighted in San Francisco in 1973. In the spring of that year, Frank Worthen, a practising Christian homosexual, rededicated his life to Christ and renounced the gay lifestyle he had indulged in for more than twenty years.

In an attempt to communicate the good news that there *is* a way out of homosexuality, Frank Worthen set up first a part-time, non-residential counselling programme, then a live-in counselling programme where individuals who had made a commitment to Christ and a commitment to come out of gayness in obedience to his Word could receive help, support, teaching and care. Homosexuals opting for this six-month period of 'treatment' live in same-sex households where they live and work together and support one another as each person seeks to overcome sexual temptation. The friendship generated in these households seems essential to their desire to find an exit from a way of life which may have become addictive. Within these groupings the person with a homosexual orientation learns to relate to individuals of both sexes in a wholesome and godly way.

To my knowledge, there is no such centre in Britain yet.[8] In the absence of such provision maybe it is time for Christian cell groups to work towards the goal of offering similar support and encouragement not just to homosexuals but to others battling against the current storm of cultural norms also?

The desire to change

But if this 'friendship therapy' is to bear fruit, the homosexual must want to change. God does not force change on us. He does point out where changes need to take place but he invites us to open the doors to change for ourselves, not to expect them to operate on automatic. As we are reminded from Holman Hunt's moving representation of Revelation 3:20, his painting of Jesus standing outside a closed, seemingly handleless door, knocking patiently, the handle is on the *inside*. The only person who can turn the handle is you.

In addition to this desire for change, the homosexual, according to Frank Worthen, needs the *belief* that change is possible.

Before homosexuality was discussed openly in Christian circles, such belief was hard to muster. Even now some homosexuals known to me find it hard to believe that they can live in Christ's strength, motivated by his Spirit rather than genital desire. But a whole series of testimonies, both from America and England, now point to the fact that God can and does change lives, including the homosexual orientation.

This fact came home to me in 1983 when I attended a conference for those involved in counselling persons with a homosexual orientation. For me, by far the most moving part of the conference occurred on the last evening when one individual after another claimed that, by the grace of God, deep wounds had been touched and healed so that radical transformations had taken place. Some former homosexuals had married and become parents. Others had been given the grace to live creative, fulfilled, single, celibate lives.

Such testimonies are now available in print. Johan van de Sluis, an ex-homosexual from Holland, tells of his own reorientation in a booklet entitled *Once a Homosexual*. He describes his feelings when, as a teenager, it seemed as though he was one of society's onlookers. 'I felt I didn't belong in the group. I was afraid of other boys and because of that I was very shy. I hated tough play. I had absolutely no interest in soccer, even though I thought I should like it.'[9] The testimony continues with an honest evaluation of his homosexual affairs and concludes with his conversion to Christianity and his struggle to shed the shackles of a now unwanted way of life.

The True Freedom Trust similarly publishes stories of those who have experienced God's intervention in their lives at the point when they despaired of ever coming to terms with their homosexuality.[10] And *Love in Action*, the live-in counselling programme I have described, makes this claim:

> Those of us who have come to Christ and renounced our gay lifestyle may have given up much that was familiar and comforting to us, but we have gained far more than we lost.[11]

The secret of such change, according to Frank Worthen, is to submit: to God and to Christian friendships. 'Submission means yielding and surrendering. . .our attitudes and independent spirit. We must build trust-relationships with God (knowing that He is at work in the long process of change) and with our brothers and sisters in Christ. . . .Submission is opening up our life to God to make the changes He wants to make. *"The depth of submission equals the heights of victory."* '[12]

Ways out of homosexuality

When we speak of escape routes from homosexuality, what we are really searching for is not a way to repress genital desire or even genital activity. That is to deal with the surface problem only and the change required is far more profound than that. What we must seek to do is to cure the homosexual condition by meeting unmet needs rather than simply try to restrict the homosexual activity which is the outcome of hidden longings. (I am not implying, by saying this, that the person with the homosexual orientation need not take responsibility for his genital activity or can claim diminished responsibility. I believe that cottaging, as seeking homosexual partners in public lavatories and other public places is called, homosexual prostitution and homosexual activity between consenting partners is wrong because such behaviour runs counter to the Bible's teaching and therefore, difficult though it is, the homosexual person should refrain from such homogenital activity. I am saying, however, that to stamp out cottaging, or, in the case of close friends, simply to stop genital play, is not a sign of complete victory. Victory comes when the *inner* needs are satisfied, met and healed.)

From talking to Frank Worthen and others whose lives are dedicated to help the homosexual find a way out of the gay lifestyle, it seems there is a route out of homosexuality. The following A – H is offered to readers who are serious about finding this escape route for themselves.

An A – H for homosexuals

The first step is to *acknowledge* the homogenital activity as sin. Whether you feel remorse is irrelevant. Apply the objective truth of the Bible to the homosexual practices I have described and recognize that, in the sight of God, these are unacceptable.

Because this is biblical, objective truth, move on to the next phase: *brokenness*. An essential ingredient of the Christian life is humbling ourselves under the mighty and loving hand of God: allowing him to break us, watching him marvel over the fragments of our brokenness, pick up the pieces and remake us in his own image.

Brokenness will be accompanied by *confession*, the facet of prayer which pours into the lap of God the fact of our failure and the sorrow we feel in failing. Confession must always lead to repentance, the *determination* to dedicate our lives, not to pleasing ourselves, but to obeying and pleasing God. But Frank Worthen emphasizes that the haul out of the gay lifestyle is a long and arduous one. 'God seldom 'ZAPs' anyone out of their old lifestyle. The Holy Spirit is gentle with us, bringing change on a daily basis, but never demanding from us behaviour that is beyond our ability to perform.'[13]

Therefore, the person struggling out of gayness must *exer-*

cise patience and seek a daily *filling of the Spirit,* whose empowering alone both motivates and equips the individual for change. And since taking even these steps will probably prove difficult, he or she will need God's *grace* in every aspect of life.

Finally, the homosexual will need to seek the kind of *healing* which I shall describe in the final chapter of this book.

How should the homosexual view himself?

If you are reading this chapter because you yourself have a homosexual orientation, it is vital that you reflect on the thesis of this chapter: that the homosexual person is a person who has been wounded in the past, a hidden orphan, one who is in transit sexually speaking. Recollect that the homosexual is a person with a great capacity for love and a deep desire and need to be loved. Remember that the homosexual is a mourner: one who is still smarting from the pain which comes to each of us when we lose someone special. In other words, remind yourself that the homosexual person, far from being the self-labelled loathsome toad he may think he is, is someone in need of a great deal of understanding, compassion and friendship. The homosexual is one with legitimate but unmet love needs which must be met, though not by eroticism, genital stimulation or orgasm.

If you have homosexual tendencies remember that you are someone who is loved with God's unending, protective love; someone who needs to be rescued by his gentle hands; someone whose inner wounds need the anointing of the oil of God's Holy Spirit.

And try to hold two things in tension: that you are loved, that you are accepted as you are, but that you will need to be changed into the likeness of Christ; that you must take full responsibility for what you do with your homosexual inclinations: use them as an occasion for genital sin or see them as a challenge to grow.

In the middle of writing this chapter, I paused for a chat to my neighbour. She showed me some bumps in the tarmac on her garden path: small, round mounds, like molehills, which are cracking the path's surface. In reply to my question,

'What is it?', she replied: 'It's thistles. They're so strong and determined, they're even penetrating the hard surface of the tarmac.'

I reflected that the homosexual condition is not unlike that tarmac on the garden path. It seems impenetrable. But when the Spirit of God moves into the hidden life underneath with all his power and healing energy, it is possible to break through; to burst into a dimension of living which had previously been an envy, but now becomes a reality.

Fear of homosexuality

And what if you are one of those people who fear that you are homosexual but are not certain? I hope I have written enough in this chapter already to encourage you not to hug this secret fear to yourself, but to share it with someone. If there is no counsellor or pastor in your area, write to the True Freedom Trust[14], and they will help you personally or put you in touch with someone near you who will offer sensitive help.

My reason for encouraging you to clarify the situation with an experienced counsellor is that, in my experience as a helper of homosexuals, many, many people fear they are homosexual when what they are encountering is the normal process of growth. Henri Nouwen puts the situation well:

> The experience of homosexual feelings in a certain period of life, or in a temporary fashion, or in certain situations, is a perfectly usual, healthy and normal thing. Involvement in a homosexual act or different homosexual acts during a period of life is not fatal in the sense that one is now doomed to be a homosexual for the rest of his life. More dangerous than the experience is the anxiety and fear related to it and the avoidance of asking for help and advice.[15]

If you suffer from the fear that you are a homosexual by orientation, seek help. Unless you do, guilt, self-hatred, anger against God will win round after round in your life. Such negatives might even push you into putting into practice what you believe yourself to be.

And if you are one of those healthy, heterosexual, outgoing types, the kind of Christian who finds the very mention of the word homosexual repulsive, may I ask you to re-evaluate your prejudiced opinion; and to place it alongside the Bible's injunction to relieve the pain of the orphan? May I encourage you to deepen your understanding of the homosexual condition: not merely to view it as genital activity which incurs the wrath of God, but to recognize the underlying pain, the festering wounds which need a touch from God; festering wounds which God might want to heal through the channel of *your* love?

Notes for chapter eleven

1. *The Gay Manifesto*, quoted by Donald Goergen in *The Sexual Celibate* (Seabury Press, 1974), p.35.
2. John White, *Eros Defiled* (IVP, 1978), p.105.
3. William F. Kraft, *Sexual Dimensions of the Celibate Life* (Gill & Macmillan, 1979), p.153.
4. Donald Goergen, *The Sexual Celibate* p.85.
5. Elizabeth R. Moberly, *Homosexuality: A New Christian Ethic* (Clarke, 1983), p.29.
6. Henri Nouwen, quoted by Donald Goergen, *The Sexual Celibate*, p.85.
7. Elizabeth Moberly, *Homosexuality*, p.30.
8. For those living in the London area, *Turning Point* now organizes groups where young people with a homosexual problem can meet together with a counsellor on a weekly basis and where individuals can receive help. For further details write to: Turning Point, PO Box 592, London SE4 1EF.
9. Johan van der Sluis, *Once a Homosexual* (Onze Weg, no date), p.4.
10. For example, *Full Freedom, A Testimony from Carole* (True Freedom Trust, no date).
11. Love in Action International, PO Box 2655, San Rafael CA94912, USA.
12. Frank Worthen, 'Steps out of Homosexuality'. Quoted in *Steps Towards Wholeness* (True Freedom Trust, 1984), p.46.
13. Frank Worthen, *Tracking the Change Process* (Love in Action duplicated article, no date).
14. True Freedom Trust, PO Box 3, Upton Wirral, Merseyside, L49 6NY.
15. Henri Nouwen, quoted by Donald Goergen in *The Sexual Celibate*, p.192.

12
Failure in Friendship

Failure in friendships of all kinds is a frequent occurrence. In particular, sexual failure takes us by surprise and dresses us down to size. A student friend of mine whom I quoted in the Preface of this book put the situation well in a letter to me once: 'How do we keep God at the centre? I vividly remember starting going out with Carole. My eyes were open. I knew all the pitfalls (I'd read about them!). God was going to stay firmly at the centre. We talked about it, even prayed about it, but in retrospect it didn't happen. The trouble was that Eros, those human feelings which are most like God's love and God's voice, seemed so much stronger, more imminent and infinitely less demanding than God and were always imperceptibly edging him out.'

This couple, like many before them and just as many since their relationship disintegrated, went further physically than either of them ever intended. Like many, many others they became riddled with guilt.

Or I think of Pamela. Pamela had been married for several years when, to her great surprise, she 'fell in love' with Joy, a woman slightly older than herself. Although neither Pamela nor Joy would have called themselves lesbians before this encounter, they both experienced comfort from the tenderness of touch and excitement from the erotic nature of their friendship. When, on one occasion, Pamela and Joy actually went to bed together and were sorely tempted to bring one another to orgasm, Pamela realized the situation was serious and reached out for help.

Again, my mind goes back to a student who asked for help

at a conference once. 'I'm always making a mess of my life and blokes' lives by going too far physically. I don't understand what makes me do it when I know I'll regret it afterwards.'

In this chapter we must address ourselves to two pressing problems. What should Christians do when they fail in friendship? What should Christians do when they fail sexually? In order to answer these questions succinctly, I propose to outline ten procedures which provide possible ways out of the guilt and oppression which plague us in the aftermath of sexual failure.

Confess

The first thing to do is to confess. Failure in friendship, painful though it is, is not the unforgivable sin. Even sexual sin is not the unforgivable sin. Whenever we become aware of failure of any kind, therefore, we must confess.

Confession is telling God the whole sordid story as we perceive it, tipping all the debris of our lives at the foot of the cross, withholding nothing from a merciful God.

For some people, it seems quite sufficient to pour out the whole sad story to God on their own, receive his forgiveness and then to bask in it. Because sexual sin scars the mind, the memory, the imagination and the body, many of us need the therapy James describes when sexual failure has caught us off our guard: 'Confess your sins to each other and pray for each other so that you may be healed' (James 5:16).

I am not suggesting that you unveil your innermost secrets before the assembled fellowship group or Bible study group. But I am seriously suggesting that, if you have confessed on your own and still feel confused, weighed down by the burden of past misdemeanours, or lack peace with God, you seek out an adult whom you trust, who is discerning, wise, prayerful, and who is capable of keeping confidences. I am also suggesting that in the presence of this trusted person, you pour your pain into the lap of God remembering that God is well able to interpret all our methods of communication: words, sighs, groans, tears and silence. Indeed, as Paul reminds us: 'The Spirit helps us in our weakness. We do not

know what we ought to pray, but the Spirit himself inter-
cedes for us with groans that words cannot express. And he
who searches our hearts knows the mind of the Spirit'
(Romans 8:26–27).

When you have acknowledged and expressed your
culpability, regret and penitence in this way, the biggest
blockage obstructing the path between you and God is
removed. Your friend now has an amazing privilege: to stand
on the authority of Jesus and declare, in his Name, that you
are 'Not guilty'. This astounding truth may trickle from your
head into your heart only very slowly, but you must try to
grasp the truth that God no longer looks on your sin but on
the crucified form of his Son, hanging on Calvary's tree in
your place. God concentrates, therefore, not on the sordid-
ness of the confession you have made, but on the fact that the
account has been settled, the price paid by the sacrifice of his
Son's life. *God* therefore declares you 'Not guilty'. God sets
you free from the death penalty and from the attending guilt.
You must therefore *go* free even if your feelings persuade you
that you are not yet free.

Believe
The second stage is to believe that the above facts about God
are true; to believe 1 John 1:9: 'If we confess our sins, he is
faithful and just and will forgive us our sins and purify us
from all unrighteousness.'

Confidence that God has forgiven us sometimes comes
only gradually, over a period of weeks or months after the
confession. You know when it has become a reality when you
can look back on the activity which grieved God and, instead
of wallowing in self-pity or self-loathing, give thanks that this
activity became a trophy of his grace rather than primarily a
sign of your disgrace. Give yourself time to realize this. Be
patient with yourself while God etches these facts on your
mind and on your heart.

Receive
When you have confessed and believed, you are free to
rejoice in God's free-flowing forgiveness. I sometimes think

of God's forgiveness as a giant waterfall which cascades down the cliff face in a hot and weary desert. I watched children bathe in such a waterfall in Israel once. They splashed in the rock-pools and refreshed themselves in the foaming spray. God delights to pour out forgiveness for us. In gratitude to him, as well as from need and in relief, take full advantage of this ever-available, renewing and renewable refreshment.

Be healed

When you have confessed, believed and received God's generous but undeserved forgiveness, you are ready to receive another love gift: the gift of healing. The sequence is not always as clear cut as this, but all the elements need to be present.

Whenever a person fails sexually, wounds are inflicted. There is the indescribable abyss of abandonment you may have fallen into, the assault on your self-worth, the searing of the conscience, the scarring of the mind. It is no accident that the Holy Spirit is often described as oil. Oil is a soothing ointment, and it contains healing properties. The prayer of healing includes the prayer that the Holy Spirit would touch and soothe and heal over the sexual sores that weep within. This healing balm is available, yet what so often happens when we feel grazed from failure is that we hide our hurts from God and try to pretend that nothing has happened. We project to the world a capable, efficient, coping image and wonder why we feel fragmented; why the hidden parts of us fall apart even though outwardly all seems well. The reason, of course, is that we are walking around with an emotional brokenness which restricts our life just as much as a broken arm or a fractured thigh.

What we must do, instead, is to expose our brokenness to the healing hand of God. Some people prefer to do this on their own. Others invite the friend or counsellor or pastor I mentioned earlier, not simply to pray for their cleansing, but for their healing. Many would use a derivation of the following prayer.

'Lord Jesus. You see where I am hurting inside. Thank you that my brokenness is not hidden from you but that you care about it. You care about me. Just as the Good Samaritan came to the wounded traveller and bound up his wounds, I ask that, by the gentle anointing of your Spirit, you would come to my inner hurts like that. Cleanse the sores. Anoint them. Bind them up. Then, would you pick me up so that I can begin living again, not in my own strength, but buoyed up with yours. I ask these things for my healing and for the glory of Jesus. Amen.'

Whenever we pray for such healing something good happens because God both hears and honours such prayer.

The healing and renewing of the mind

But healing is bigger and broader than the canvas I have spread before you so far. It includes the healing and the renewing of the mind. Whenever we fail, Satan hovers around the scene of the crash and whispers subtle, condemnatory lies. 'What a hypocrite you are. You can't be forgiven for that. It's too late now. You've forfeited God's love but it doesn't matter because his love is a strait-jacket, restrictive love anyway. You've failed so many times, it's no good confessing again – go out and enjoy yourself.' And our tired brain believes this voice; even confuses it with the voice of the Holy Spirit.

We must remind ourselves at such times that the Holy Spirit convicts. He never condemns. Learn to recognize the source of these condemnatory voices, therefore: Satan. Stand against him and stand against his lies, refusing to believe them. The friend praying for you can do this with you. Tune out the lying tongue. Tune into the truth by asking, 'What does Jesus say about me?' Read his Word, the Bible, to rediscover there the consoling assurance that your failure does not erase his love. Read Psalm 51, for example, and make it your personal prayer.

The healing of the memories

Even so, God's healing work may not yet be completed. At

the beginning of this chapter I gave a thumbnail sketch of Pam's story. When Pamela came to me for help we talked about her childhood. As we did, it became apparent that she had never really felt loved by her mother. She could rationalize and conclude, 'She *must* have loved me – she sacrificed so much for me.' But she could not recall ever feeling the full warmth of the mother-love she had pined for.

We decided, therefore, to bring this lack of love to God and to ask him to fill up some of the love-gaps which yawned inside Pam.

As we prayed, Pam seemed to see a picture of herself as though she were watching a replay of her life on video-cassette. She was a baby sucking her mother's breasts. But the breasts were empty. Pamela experienced again the pain and frustration of sucking in air when she needed and expected milk. That picture seemed to symbolize the entire mother-Pamela relationship.

But as we continued to pray and to expose this deep emptiness to God, Pam seemed to see a picture of Jesus coming to her, the vulnerable infant. He held her. She snuggled into him. She gripped his big but loving finger. He bottle-fed her with warm, nourishing milk and his holding of her was tender, like the motherly love Pamela had always longed for. And Pamela sensed an inner harmony dislodge the turmoil which had once wracked her emotions.

That day, Pamela realized that, even though the relationship with her mother had lacked certain ingredients of the emotional and physical sustenance every child needs, nevertheless Jesus, the source of all true love and sustenance, was attending to every deep-seated need of hers. Indeed, the love of Jesus seemed to fill the gaps inside her in an almost physical way. This is how she described it. 'One minute my life seemed to be like an empty well. The next minute I watched the water-level rising. I knew, as I watched, that this was the rising level of God's love. It was wonderful to feel full rather than empty.'

I have related this account of Pamela's healing in detail to demonstrate and underline the fact that God's Spirit and love can seep into the crevices of our being; can even touch and heal those places where we have been wounded or neglected in the past.

This good news is of great importance to the person with the homosexual orientation, because it means that through the prayer of inner healing, the Holy Spirit can begin to meet and compensate for some of the lack of love in the past which forms the major blockage to full sexual, emotional and spiritual maturation. This good news is of importance to heterosexuals also: to the girl who, despite all her good intentions, lived promiscuously; to the young man who admitted that he turned to sex entertainment (by which he meant blue movies, strip shows and girlie magazines), in an attempt to buy an intimacy he had never had. It is good news because it means that there is a love which can reach right down to the forlorn and loveless child who dwells within such persons, and provide the necessary love, a love that can even be felt. I have not only witnessed this quiet miracle taking place, I have also seen the effects such healing has on relationships. Take Pamela, whom I mentioned earlier, for example. Her relationship with Joy was transformed. In a gradual way, it became healing and wholesome, and mutually supportive.

Healing is gradual

'In a gradual way. . . .' The healing I have described is effective, but its long-term consequences unfold only gradually. When you think about the nature of such healing, this is hardly surprising. Through it, the person whose growth was stunted through deprivation in the past is touched in the place of hurt. If, like Pamela, that hurt stems back to infancy, it follows that a great deal of learning has yet to take place: the learning we all have to absorb through the natural maturing process. That is why change in many of us is so slow. It is not that God is inactive but rather that he allows us the luxury of slow learning. Instead of waving a magic wand, like a divine Mary Poppins, and watching everything leap into place immediately, God respects our privacy and individuality and simply provides us with the ingredients for the growth which will result, eventually, in full maturity.

When we have received such prayer, therefore, we should

look for every sign of change but not become despondent when such changes seem slow and when, at times, we seem to take three steps forwards and four backwards. Neither should we feel embarrassed about asking for prayer for such hurts more than once. There is great value in what Francis MacNutt calls 'soaking prayer': praying for someone regularly until the healing work is complete.

Forgive

But I do not want to give the impression that God does all the work. Some needy people seem to present themselves and their problem to God, wait for his prescription and the medicine and expect the magic of healing. God's healing is not like that. It always involves our co-operation. And one of the ways we can co-operate with the Holy Spirit of God is to forgive.

The reason I mention this is because, whenever a person has been deprived of love in the past in the way I have described, a certain amount of resentment, bitterness and anger collects, like pockets of poison, in that person's life. As the young man whose inner hurts prompted him to seek intimacy through pornography admitted, 'Hate would not be too strong a word. At times I really hate my mother.'

Forgiveness for such people involves setting the parent figure free with a deliberate act of the will. Take this same young man, for example. We encouraged him to recall, to the full, his parents' failure in their loving of him, then to visualize them standing at the foot of the cross with him and the dying Jesus, and to pray a derivation of the prayer Jesus prayed from that same cross: 'Father, forgive them. They don't know what they're doing.'

Such a prayer is wonderfully liberating both for the injured person who prays it and for the person who inflicted the pain in the first place. They are both set free from the bondage such negatives place people in; free to make more effective and healing relationships.

Co-operate

Such prayer for forgiveness does not only apply to those who know they have been wounded in the past. It applies equally to those who have failed in friendship in the present, and to those who have failed sexually. They, too, must co-operate with the transforming Holy Spirit.

Let me explain what I mean by this. It often happens that when friendships founder or when we have compromised our own sex standards, we either condemn ourselves or blame the other person involved. We have already noted the vital part confession plays, and that honest confession is always followed by God's freely given forgiveness. What we now have to do is to forgive ourselves and the person who has wronged or hurt us.

'How do you do that?' The girl who asked me that question had been raped after putting herself in a compromising situation. The process is simple but costly. It involves remembering the guilt and recalling the pain. Without ever denying that what actually happened did in fact take place, you ask two far-reaching questions: '*Will* I forgive myself?' '*Will* I forgive him/her?'

The temptation, when faced with those questions, is to bleat: 'I can't.' Gradually we learn that 'I can't' is not an adequate answer, it is an excuse. There are only two possible replies to the questions above: 'I will' or 'I won't'. When faced with them, therefore, we must struggle and strive, wait and pray for the will to be willing to embark on the most exhilarating part of the journey: to forgive. When our will has been marshalled into submission, we then recall the incident which still causes pain or shame and we pray our own version of Jesus' prayer on the cross: 'Father, forgive them, they didn't know what they were doing.' 'Father, forgive *me*, I didn't realize the full implication of what I was doing.'

This prayer is liberating because, when we utter it, God performs deep surgery on us. Just as we forgive the former friend who wronged us, so God forgives us. He comes to us. He lances the abscess where the pus and poison of resentment and bitterness have collected. He replaces these negatives with overflowing love: tenderness, compassion, understanding. By helping us to see the horrifying situation from the other person's point of view, he encourages us to have true compassion for them.

Receive God's grace

But what if we fail frequently? What if, like the girl who wrote to me on one occasion, you have failed many partners? 'Each time I came to God for forgiveness and had known forgiveness by him. Yet each time it made a difference for a few weeks only. . . .I really don't know what's going on in me. It's not my intentions that are wrong, just what I do.'

We must never become *blasé* and take God's grace for granted. But neither must we despair. Rather, we will ask God to apply his blood to the weeds which ravage our lives. Let me explain what I mean.

For the past year, a huge weed has grown up next to the honeysuckle which I am trying to train to grow around my dining-room window. When I asked my husband to cut it down, he looked at the girth of the trunk of the bush-like weed, and laughed. 'I couldn't possibly cut that down without damaging the wall.' Scornfully, I watched him water the offending weed with a liberal supply of ultra-strong weed killer. A week later, to my utter amazement and chagrin, the once upstanding weed had withered. It has now shrivelled and died.

I am not implying that a magic solution can be applied to the soul which will eradicate our propensity to sin sexually or to fail in friendship. As I underlined in chapter six, we are not God's robots, nor God's puppets, but responsible adults capable of making choices. But neither do I want to suggest that we must grit our teeth and conquer alone. To learn to love, as we have noted all through this book, is to come to terms with a complex art form. As Walter Trobisch reminds us so aptly: 'Love is a feeling to be learned *by grace*'.[1] Those of us who know we are weak, who have experienced the humiliation of failure, need a liberal sprinkling of the grace of God to saturate this area of our lives.

Refocus

Confess. Believe in the generosity of God. Receive his forgiveness. Accept his healing. Tune out, and drive out, satanic whispers. Then refocus.

It is easy to wallow in self-pity or remorse or in guilt feelings. This does no-one any good and is, in fact, piling one sin upon another. Turn your back on the past and drink in, instead, the sheer wonder of the love of God. Rejoice in it. Be awed by the sheer generosity of it. Wonder at the vitality of it as you do when energy returns to your body after an illness. This may take weeks, rather than minutes, but gradually refrain from wallowing in your own weakness and fill your horizon with the realization of God's overwhelming love, which eradicates sin.

Realize that God is bigger than your mistakes

Next, marvel at the miracle-working nature of God; at the realization that God is bigger than our mistakes. It often happens that the memories of our sexual misdemeanours crush us: 'I've scarred my girlfriend for life'; 'I should never have gone out with a non-Christian. What kind of witness have I been? How will he ever understand God's love after what I've done to him?'

Thanks be to God, this failure is not the end of the story. God is bigger than our mistakes. He does not have to unpick our lives, or go back to the dropped stitch. No. Instead, out of the greatness of his love for us, he weaves our mistakes into the fabric of our lives and even makes them beautiful. Our responsibility, therefore, is to acknowledge where we failed others; then, as though Jesus was in the room with us, to bring the messy situation, and particularly the wronged person, into his all-capable, all-loving hands and to leave them there.

It often helps, in this prayer of relinquishment, if someone else is present when the final handing-over happens. You can pray together that God will take full responsibility for the friend you failed. If ever you have occasion to doubt that you completed this task, your confidante can remind you that they witnessed the handing-over ceremony.

Repent

But all that I have said so far will bear little fruit unless repentance reshapes our lives. Anthony Bloom says this of repentance: 'We should never lure ourselves into imagining that to lament one's past is an act of repentance. It is part of it, of course, but repentance remains unreal and barren so long as it has not led us into doing the will of the Father. We have a tendency to think that it should result in fine emotions and we are quite often satisfied with emotions instead of real, deep changes.'[2]

Jim Wallis puts it another way. 'Repentance is seeing our sin and turning from it: faith is seeing Jesus and turning towards him.'[3] Just as on Easter Day, Mary was challenged to turn her back on the grave which once entombed Jesus and to fix her gaze on him, so we are called to turn our backs on all that once held us captive and to focus our love on him: to make him the pivot around which our world revolves. Until we have done this, until he is re-enthroned, all our weeping and wailing, confession and chastising will be of no avail. We have to be changed by Christ from the inside out.

But when that miracle called repentance does begin to reshape our lives, something astonishingly beautiful happens. It is as though God creates from the seeming ruin of our lives a priceless pearl. A pearl is the result of an accident. A pearl is the result of grit in the oyster. A pearl is one of nature's glorious 'mistakes'. A pearl is precious.

And such, by the grace of God, are we, not in spite of our misdemeanours but because of the overwhelming goodness which is God. As I have emphasized in my book, *Growing into Love*[4], and as Walter Trobisch reminds us, 'There is no life so messed up that he cannot bring it in order. He can even make done things undone by his forgiveness. For this is what forgiveness means: to make done things undone.'[5]

This last chapter of this book was almost completed when a student came to see me to talk over her seeming inability to make lasting relationships. As we talked, despair in her turned to hope. God seemed to remind us of the example Jesus set us. He seemed to remind us, too, of the encouraging picture of ourselves which is painted in Hebrews 12:

Since we have such a huge crowd of men of faith watching
us from the grandstands, let us strip off anything that
slows us down or holds us back, and especially those sins
that wrap themselves so tightly around our feet and trip us
up; and let us run with patience the particular race that
God has set before us.

Keep your eyes on Jesus, our leader and instruc-
tor. . . .Look after each other so that not one of you will
fail to find God's best blessings (Hebrews 12:1–2,15 LB).

These are favourite verses of mine. They remind me of the
Olympic Games or of Wimbledon. They remind me that we
are the players in the centre of the arena and that this huge
crowd in the grandstands, which includes God, is on our
side, willing us to win. Whenever we succeed, they roar their
approval. Whenever we fail, they call out: 'Come on. You
can do it. We believe in you.' And whenever we pluck up the
courage to begin again, they show that they are on our side:
'Keep it up. We're willing you to make it.'

Making creative relationships is one of the biggest challenges that ever faces a human being. We never fully gradu-
ate. Nevertheless, human friendship is one of God's best
blessings. However much we fail, therefore, we must never
stop trying to make all sorts of Christlike friendships.

Notes for chapter twelve

1. Walter Trobisch, *Love is a Feeling to be Learned* (IVP, 1974), p.32 (italics
   mine).
2. Anthony Bloom, *Living Prayer* (Libra, 1973), p.66.
3. Jim Wallis, *The Call to Conversion* (Lion, 1981), p.5.
4. See 'Treating the Indelible Stain' by Joyce Huggett in *Growing into Love*
   (IVP, 1982).
5. Walter Trobisch, *Love is a feeling. . .*, p.31.